HIST

D0407052

1

WESTWARD EXPANSION AND MANIFEST DESTINY IN AMERICAN HISTORY

Other titles *in American History*

JUN 1 3 2001

IN
AMERICAN
HISTORY

WESTWARD EXPANSION AND MANIFEST DESTINY IN AMERICAN HISTORY

Richard Worth

3 1336 05456 2567

Enslow Publishers, Inc.

40 Industrial Road	PO Box 38
Box 398	Aldershot
Berkeley Heights, NJ 07922	Hants GU12 6BP
USA	UK

http://www.enslow.com

Copyright © 2001 by Richard Worth

All rights reserved.

No part of this book may be reproduced by any means
without the written permission of the publisher.

Library of Congress Cataloging-in-Publication Data

Worth, Richard.
    Westward expansion and manifest destiny in American history / Richard
Worth.
        p. cm. — (In American history)
    Includes bibliographical references (p.) and index.
    ISBN 0-7660-1457-6
    1. United States—Territorial expansion—Juvenile literature. [1. United
States—Territorial expansion.] I. Title. II. Series.
    E179.5 .W66 2001
    973—dc21
                                                    00-009280

Printed in the United States of America

10 9 8 7 6 5 4 3 2 1

To Our Readers: All Internet addresses in this book were active and appropriate
at the time we went to press. Any comments or suggestions can be sent by e-mail
to Comments@enslow.com or to the address on the back cover.

Illustration Credits: Enslow Publishers, Inc., pp. 14, 17, 38, 69, 92,
98; Library of Congress, pp. 25, 27, 30, 33, 34, 44, 54, 61, 66, 68, 71,
74, 76, 77, 80, 81, 83, 99; National Archives, pp. 101, 102; National
Park Service, p. 39; Reproduced from the *Dictionary of American
Portraits*, Published by Dover Publications, Inc., in 1967, pp. 8, 10, 15.

Cover Illustration: Library of Congress; National Archives;
Reproduced from the *Dictionary of American Portraits*, Published by
Dover Publications, Inc., in 1967.

★ CONTENTS ★

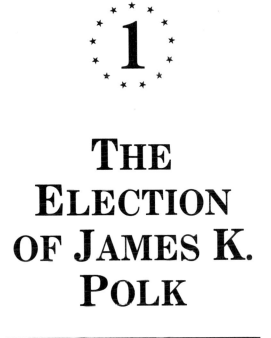

THE ELECTION OF JAMES K. POLK

James Knox Polk began his political career during the 1820s in Tennessee. His family, looking for new land and prosperity, had moved there when James was still a child. They were part of a great western migration bringing thousands of settlers to the Tennessee Valley—a westward movement that would eventually plant American homesteaders along the banks of the Rio Grande in Texas and the shores of the Pacific Ocean. Polk caught the spirit of the westward movement when he was a boy. It would continue to influence him when he became a politician.

At a time when relatively few young men went to college, Polk entered the University of North Carolina at Chapel Hill in 1815. He joined the debating society and learned to be an effective speaker. This would help him achieve success in politics—first as a Tennessee state legislator in 1823, then as a congressman two years later. Along the way, he made a close friend of General Andrew Jackson—also from Tennessee. In 1828, Polk campaigned vigorously for Jackson, who was

Andrew Jackson is often considered the first common man to become the United States president.

elected president. Jackson was the first political leader from the West to reach the White House. President Jackson frequently turned to Polk for advice. Polk was one of the president's most loyal supporters in Congress on issues involving westward expansion.

During Jackson's administration, American settlers were moving west into Texas, which was then part of Mexico. They established homes, carved out plantations, and brought the institution of slavery to the region. The settlers formed a tight-knit group. They maintained their identity as Americans and had a fierce desire to govern themselves. In 1835, they rebelled against Mexico, declared their independence, and asked to be annexed, or become part of the United States. President Jackson strongly favored annexation, but he was opposed by Northerners in Congress, who feared the admission of another slave state. Nothing more was done, and Texas remained an independent republic until 1844.

The Election of 1844

Polk believed strongly in admitting Texas as a state. In Congress, he had been a strong supporter of westward expansion. Two of his cousins had fought in the war to win Texas independence. As a plantation owner and slaveholder, he also sympathized with the other Southerners who had settled in Texas. Polk was a prominent member of the Democratic party and he confidently aspired to be the party's choice for vice president in the 1844 election. Many party leaders believed that Polk, a Southerner, would balance the ticket headed by former President Martin Van Buren from New York. (Van Buren had served as president from 1837 to 1841.) Both Van Buren and Polk were strongly endorsed by Andrew Jackson.

Meanwhile, support had begun to grow for the idea of admitting Texas as a state. Annexation rapidly became one of the major issues of the 1844 election. Van Buren said he was opposed to the annexation of Texas because he felt it might start a war with Mexico, which still claimed Texas as its own territory. Jackson strongly disagreed with Van Buren. Jackson began looking for someone else to represent the Democrats in the coming election.

Polk was summoned to Jackson's home in Tennessee. The old ex-president was living in retirement, but he still had a lot of influence in the

Democratic party. Polk and Jackson talked about the upcoming election, and Jackson was assured that Polk supported Texas annexation.

After the meeting, Polk wrote a friend that Jackson "thinks the candidate for the Presidency should be an annexation man and reside in the Southwest, and he openly expresses (what I assure you I had never for a moment contemplated) the opinion that I would be the most available man. . . ."[1] Polk's position on Texas had helped him receive Jackson's support.

Eventually, Polk defeated Van Buren for the presidential nomination. The Democrats called for the annexation of Texas as soon as possible. Later, Polk went on to defeat Whig candidate Henry Clay in the presidential election of 1844. Clay did not support admitting Texas as a state.

Polk believed his election as president had happened largely because he supported annexing

James Knox Polk won the presidency after a campaign that stressed support for expansion in the West.

Texas. Indeed, many Americans seemed to support the expansion of the United States. Polk saw himself as their spokesman.

During the presidential campaign of 1844, no one used the term *Manifest Destiny* to describe territorial expansion. This term was coined in 1845 by John L. O'Sullivan, editor of *The United States Magazine and Democratic Review*. O'Sullivan, a strong Democrat, believed that the hand of God had directed Americans to spread across the continent. God willed that America should expand to its natural boundaries— from the Atlantic Ocean in the East to the Rio Grande and the Pacific Ocean in the West. Manifest Destiny seemed to give the divine stamp of approval to westward expansion. As America expanded, it would create new areas for settlement by people living in the eastern

SOURCE DOCUMENT

. . . THE REPUBLIC OF TEXAS HAS MADE KNOWN HER DESIRE TO COME INTO OUR UNION. . . . TEXAS WAS ONCE A PART OF OUR COUNTRY—WAS UNWISELY CEDED AWAY TO A FOREIGN POWER—IS NOW INDEPENDENT, AND POSSESSES AN UNDOUBTED RIGHT TO DISPOSE OF A PART OR THE WHOLE OF HER TERRITORY. . . . I REGARD THE QUESTION OF THE ANNEXATION AS BELONGING EXCLUSIVELY TO THE UNITED STATES AND TEXAS. THEY ARE INDEPENDENT POWERS COMPETENT TO CONTRACT, AND FOREIGN NATIONS HAVE NO RIGHT TO INTERFERE WITH THEM. . . .[2]

In his inaugural address on March 4, 1845, President Polk showed his support for the annexation of Texas.

United States. Those Americans who had been unsuccessful running farms and businesses could move westward and try again. Manifest Destiny was part of the westward movement that had brought Polk and his family to Tennessee. Men like Polk, who were strong believers in expansion, also strongly supported the concept of Manifest Destiny. It reflected a growing national confidence in the ability of Americans to overcome any obstacle to make their country the greatest power on the continent of North America.

Manifest Destiny would be the dominant theme of President Polk's new administration. It would propel the United States into a war with Mexico. The Mexicans controlled the territory along the Rio Grande and the Pacific Ocean, including present-day Texas, New Mexico, Arizona, Nevada, California, Utah, and Colorado. Polk believed this territory should form America's natural boundaries. Polk and the idea of Manifest Destiny would also bring about tense negotiations between the United States and Great Britain over which country had the right to the Oregon Territory in the northwest. Ultimately, Polk would acquire huge western territories, and the power of Manifest Destiny would shape the modern United States.

TEXAS AND THE WESTERN FRONTIER

Happy America!" Dr. David Ramsay, a southern political leader, wrote in 1778, "whose expanse of territory to the west is sufficient to provide lands to thousands and millions of the virtuous peasants who now groan under tyranny and oppression in three quarters of the globe. . . ."[1] Many people were lured to America by the western frontier. It offered them a second chance. Here settlers found a vast wilderness. They could clear a few acres of woodland, build a new house, and start a farm for themselves and their families.

When Europeans first settled North America during the 1600s, the frontier lay along the Atlantic seaboard. But as more immigrants came from Europe, the coastline seemed to grow too crowded—at least for some. These hardy adventurers pushed farther inland, paddling their canoes along the great rivers of the interior. They established trading posts with various American Indian tribes and eventually built new settlements at places like Pittsburgh on the Ohio River.

The Westward Movement

In 1783, in the Treaty of Paris that ended the American Revolution, Great Britain granted the United States an enormous western region. It stretched from the Ohio River to the Mississippi River. Suddenly, America's boundaries stretched all the way from the Atlantic Ocean to the Mississippi.

Of course, much of this area was still inhabited by American Indians such as the Creek and Shawnee.

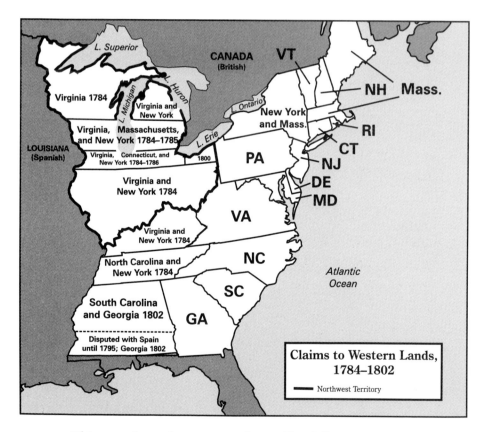

This map shows the territory claimed by different states and ceded the United States after the end of the revolution.

Some tribes eventually signed peace treaties with American negotiators and moved away. But others were not willing to give up their lands without a fight. They were encouraged by the British, who controlled Canada. Great Britain wanted to carry on a profitable fur trade in the area. It hoped to stop the westward expansion of the United States. But the tribes proved no match for American forces led by General Anthony Wayne. He defeated an army of two thousand American Indian warriors in northwest Ohio at the Battle of Fallen Timbers in 1794. The next year, they signed the Treaty of Greenville. In doing so, they gave up a vast territory that would later become part of the states of Ohio and Indiana.

In the south, settlers had also been pushing back the boundaries of the frontier. During the 1770s, Daniel Boone had carved the Wilderness Road through the Cumberland Gap—a path in the Appalachian

Frontiersman Daniel Boone became famous for cutting a path to the West and establishing the first white settlement in Kentucky.

Mountains. This mountain range stretches from north to south through the present-day states of New York, Tennessee, Virginia, Georgia, Pennsylvania, and Alabama. Beyond the Cumberland Gap, Boone established Boonesborough on the Kentucky River.

After the American Revolution, homesteaders poured along the Wilderness Road to the rich bluegrass country of Kentucky and Tennessee. They were lured by cheap land where they could grow corn and tobacco. But they also met hostile American Indian tribes supported by Spain. The Spanish held an empire in North America that included Louisiana, Florida, and a vast wilderness west of the Mississippi River. The Spanish believed the American Indians could stop expansion by American settlers and help protect the Spanish territories.

American settlers in Ohio had hoped to ship their farm produce from the Spanish port of New Orleans to customers in Europe. But Spain closed the lower Mississippi River and New Orleans to American commerce. Spain wanted to prevent the growth of American commerce and power, which might threaten Spanish territories. Finally, in 1795, the Spanish government signed the Pinckney Treaty. Americans agreed to halt their westward expansion and not to push into Spanish territories in Florida and Louisiana. In return, Spain agreed to open the entire Mississippi River, guaranteeing that American goods could be shipped from New Orleans to Europe. Spain also promised to try to keep the American Indian tribes from attacking American colonial settlements.

The Louisiana Purchase

Events in Europe, however, changed the situation along the American frontier. At the beginning of the nineteenth century, French leader Napoleon Bonaparte forced the weak Spanish government to turn over New Orleans and a vast portion of the Louisiana Territory west of the Mississippi to France. Bonaparte hoped to build a powerful empire in America. President Thomas Jefferson saw French control of New Orleans as a threat to the government of the United States. "There is on the globe one spot the possessor of which is our

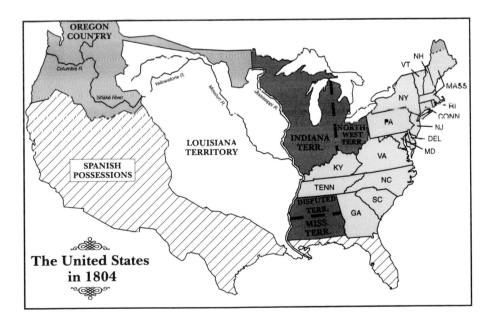

The 1803 Louisiana Purchase nearly doubled the territory of the United States.

natural and habitual enemy," Jefferson wrote. "It is New Orleans, through which the produce of three-eighths of our territory must pass to market. . . . France, placing herself in that door, assumes to us the attitude of defiance. . . ."[2]

Jefferson wanted to negotiate with Napoleon to buy the port of New Orleans. Meanwhile, French plans for starting an empire in America were changing. Napoleon had decided to concentrate his efforts in Europe, where he hoped to invade England and conquer Austria and Prussia. Instead of simply selling the port of New Orleans, the French offered to hand over the entire Louisiana Territory to the United States. This was a total of more than 800,000 square miles. In 1803, the United States paid $15 million for the Louisiana Territory.

This addition almost doubled the size of the United States. Its borders now stretched from the Mississippi River to the Rocky Mountains and northward almost to the present border with Canada. Some Americans, however, opposed the Louisiana Purchase. They believed the United States already had enough land and not enough financial resources to safely pay for any more. But President Jefferson was intent on exploring the new territory so it could eventually be opened for settlement.

In 1803, Jefferson sent out an expedition led by Meriwether Lewis and William Clark. The Lewis and Clark expedition charted the Louisiana Territory and determined that an overland route could be developed

---

SOURCE DOCUMENT

ARTICLE I

. . . THE FIRST CONSUL OF THE FRENCH REPUBLIC
DESIRING TO GIVE TO THE UNITED STATES A STRONG PROOF
OF HIS FRIENDSHIP, DOTH HEREBY CEDE TO THE SAID
UNITED STATES, IN THE NAME OF THE FRENCH REPUBLIC,
FOREVER AND IN FULL SOVEREIGNTY, THE SAID TERRITORY
[LOUISIANA], WITH ALL ITS RIGHTS AND APPURTENANCES,
AS FULLY AND IN THE SAME MANNER AS THEY HAVE BEEN
ACQUIRED BY THE FRENCH REPUBLIC. . . .[3]

*In the Louisiana Purchase treaty, France ceded some
828,000 square miles of territory to the United States.*

to the Pacific Coast so settlers might eventually be able
to move there.

The War of 1812

Although this enormous wilderness offered almost
limitless possibilities for expansion, Americans were
focused on other issues. Spain still seemed to pose a
threat from its territory in Florida. In 1810 and 1812,
President James Madison moved troops into parts of
West Florida. This upset the Creek Indian tribe. The
Creek began attacking white settlements in the area.
Finally, in 1814, an army under the command of
Andrew Jackson defeated the Creek at the Battle of
Horseshoe Bend in the present state of Alabama. The
Creek agreed to make peace. They signed over a large
area of land in Georgia and Mississippi, which was

opened to whites for settlement. Eventually, other American Indian tribes also signed peace treaties and moved westward.

The victory at Horseshoe Bend had occurred during the War of 1812, which pitted American armies against the forces of Great Britain. The war had begun because Great Britain, which was at war with France, refused to let neutral American ships trade with the French. The British stopped American ships and captured American seamen, forcing them to join the British Navy.

In 1814, near the end of the war, the British threatened New Orleans. General Jackson moved his army south to defend the port city. Here, in 1815, he won a decisive victory over a large British army. The war had actually ended by this point, but news of the peace treaty had not yet reached the United States. Still, the victory instantly turned Jackson into an American hero. New Orleans was secure.

Meanwhile, along the northern frontier, the American Indian tribes in western Ohio and Michigan had also been defeated. Although the United States gained no territory as a result of the War of 1812, it secured its independence from Great Britain, and the defeat of the American Indian tribes cleared the way for western expansion.

Transportation Helps the March West

Following the War of 1812, American settlers streamed west. Improvements in transportation helped make this migration possible. In 1825, the Erie Canal opened. The canal linked the Hudson River in eastern New York State with Lake Erie in western New York. From here, settlers could travel westward along the other Great Lakes to the present-day states of Michigan, Indiana, and Illinois.

In addition, new roads were completed to take people westward. The National Road, for example, stretched from Cumberland, Maryland, into Ohio. Not only could homesteaders travel west along it, but herds of cattle were driven over the road from farms in the West to markets in the East.

Along the Mississippi River, farmers shipped their produce to New Orleans on rafts and flatboats. Robert Fulton had launched his steamboat on the Hudson River in 1807. A few years later, the first steamboat sailed along the Mississippi. Steamboats carried not only produce, but passengers as well. As steamboats increased in number, they began to offer travelers many luxuries. In 1826, one traveler described the

> splendid cabin, richly carpeted, its finishing of mahogany, its mirrors and fine furniture, its bar-room, and sliding tables, to which eighty passengers can sit down with comfort. The fare is sumptuous . . . far exceeding that of taverns in general . . . you are sweeping along for many leagues . . . where either shore is boundless and pathless wilderness.[4]

That wilderness gradually was being transformed. In 1793, a Connecticut inventor named Eli Whitney had developed the cotton gin. This invention made the production of cotton much faster and easier. The cotton gin separated the seed from the fluffy cotton. A hand-operated gin could clean fifty times as much cotton in a day as a human being. A steam-operated gin could clean one thousand pounds a day.[5] The cotton gin helped make possible the tremendous expansion of cotton plantations in the South. Many plantations were established in the Gulf Coast states of Alabama, Mississippi, and Louisiana. With the growth of the plantations came the expansion of slavery. Southern plantation owners relied on large groups of African-American slaves to work their plantations.

Because the plantation system was so successful, Southerners wanted to expand it even farther. They intended to push the plantation system and the institution of slavery westward into the territory of Texas.

The Development of Texas

President Thomas Jefferson believed that all the land south to the Rio Grande was part of the Louisiana Purchase. This included the area known as Texas, which Jefferson thought France had controlled and given to the United States as part of Louisiana. Spain, on the other hand, claimed that Texas was not part of Louisiana, but part of the Spanish Empire in North America. This included what is now New Mexico, Arizona, and California. Finally, in 1819, Secretary of State John Quincy Adams signed a treaty with the Spanish government. Spain realized that it was not powerful enough to continue to defend Florida, so

SOURCE DOCUMENT

ARTICLE II.

His Catholic Majesty cedes to the United States, in full property and sovereignty, all the territories which belong to him, situated to the eastward of the Mississippi, known by the name of East and West Florida. The adjacent islands dependent on said provinces, all public lots and squares, vacant lands, public edifices, fortifications, barracks, and other buildings, which are not private property, archives and documents which relate directly to the property and sovereignty of the said provinces, are included in this article.[6]

The Adams-Onis Treaty gave the United States title to disputed areas of Florida.

Spain gave it to the United States. In return, the American government recognized the Spanish right to Texas.

The Spanish Empire, with its center at Mexico City, had been established in the 1500s. Texas was far removed from Mexico City and had always been very sparsely settled. During the nineteenth century, the Spanish government decided that it needed to attract new settlers if it hoped to hold the territory against hostile Indian tribes. One man who was interested in starting a settlement in Texas was Moses Austin.

During the 1790s, Austin had moved to Missouri. Missouri had been part of the Spanish Louisiana empire until it was given to France and later to the

United States under the terms of the Louisiana Purchase. Austin had been loyal to the Spanish authorities while living in their territory. They were ready to welcome him as a settler in Texas. In 1820, Austin was ready to move to Texas, but he did not live long enough to establish a settlement.

His son, Stephen, however, met with the Spanish government and selected an area in which to lay out a new community. Austin was particularly impressed with the fertile farmland along the Brazos and Colorado rivers in east Texas. In 1821, colonists led by Stephen Austin began arriving. They were given cheap land in return for swearing "a solemn oath of fidelity . . . to be faithful vassals of His Most Catholic Majesty, to act in obedience to all laws of Spain. . . ."[7] Cheap land was enough to lure some Americans away from their homeland to become citizens of Mexico.

The Americans who moved to Texas began to carve out plantations. The land along the Brazos was excellent for growing cotton. By 1825, the population included almost eighteen hundred settlers from the United States. Of these, more than four hundred were slaves.[8] The American newcomers had no intention of adopting the customs and language of Spanish Mexico. They kept their own language and religion, and traded almost exclusively with the United States instead of with the Spanish Empire. An American settlement was growing within the empire. This would eventually lead to serious conflict.

Known as the Father of Texas, Stephen Austin led Americans to settle in Texas under Spanish rule, and later encouraged many more to fight Mexico to make Texas independent.

Tensions Begin to Grow

In 1821, Mexico revolted against Spain. Two years later, it established a republic. Although Mexico had freed itself from the power of one nation, it now faced the United States, which was even more powerful. The relationship between Mexico and the United States was bound to be very difficult for at least two reasons.

The first was that a large body of Americans, primarily in the Southwest, were expansionist. They wanted Texas and all the land west to the Pacific Ocean for the United States. The second trouble was that almost all educated Mexicans hated, distrusted, or feared the rapidly growing power of their northern neighbor.[9]

This situation grew worse as the number of American settlers in Texas increased. By 1830, Americans outnumbered Mexicans in Texas by at least ten to one. This led the government in Mexico City to ban any further immigration from the United States. This so-called Decree of April 6, 1830, also imposed new taxes on the American settlers.

Meanwhile, the government of Mexico was going through a major change. In 1829, Spain had tried to recapture its empire. The invasion was beaten back by a Mexican army under the command of Antonio López de Santa Anna. General Santa Anna became a hero in the new Mexican republic. Eventually, he took control of the government. Santa Anna ruled as a dictator.

After the passage of the Decree of April 6, 1830, Stephen Austin went to Mexico City to try to have the decree removed. Austin and other political leaders of Texas wanted immigration to be resumed so Texans could continue to develop new towns and plantations. Instead of granting Austin's requests, however, Santa Anna had him arrested in early 1834. To Santa Anna, Austin and his associates posed too big a threat to the Mexican government.

Austin was released the following year and traveled to New Orleans. There, he invited Americans to come to Texas and fight in the war of Texas independence that he knew was about to begin. He hoped that the war would make Texas part of the United States, where the rights of people to develop new settlements would be protected.

Meanwhile, the Mexican government began sending troops into Texas under the command of General Martín Perfecto de Cos. He had made his headquarters at San

General Antonio López de Santa Anna gained control of the Mexican government after he helped free it from Spanish rule. He opposed American interference with any Mexican territory.

Antonio, in southern Texas. General Cos split his forces between the town itself and an old mission that had been turned into a fortress. It was known as the Alamo.

A militia gathered outside. Among the militia were some Texas settlers as well as men from the United States who had answered Stephen Austin's call to arms. Although the Texans were heavily outnumbered by General Cos's troops, they decided to attack the Mexicans. A house-to-house battle began in San Antonio. It lasted several days. The Texans killed enough Mexicans to convince General Cos to surrender on December 10, 1835. San Antonio and the Alamo now belonged to the Texans.

Remember the Alamo

The army that had won the battle at San Antonio was not a force of trained soldiers. Its men were just volunteers. After their victory, they began to drift away and return to their homes. Only a small force of about one hundred men was left to guard the Alamo.

Meanwhile, General Santa Anna was marching toward San Antonio with a powerful army of more than six thousand, including a large force of cavalry and heavy artillery. Santa Anna had wasted no time. He left Mexico City for San Luis Potosi, where he put together his army. Then he moved north to Saltillo, arriving in January. There, his army spent three weeks on training maneuvers. Finally, Santa Anna began the

365-mile journey across the Rio Grande to San Antonio and the Alamo. He and his troops arrived on February 23, 1836.[10]

The man responsible for dealing with Santa Anna's large army was General Sam Houston, commander of the tiny Texas forces. Houston had grown up in Virginia and Tennessee and had fought with General Andrew Jackson at the Battle of Horseshoe Bend. During the 1820s, Houston was elected to Congress. He later gave up his seat to make a successful run for governor of Tennessee. James K. Polk was chosen by the voters to fill Houston's position as congressman. After serving as governor, Houston eventually left Tennessee and moved to Texas. There, he won a reputation as a skilled politician and leader.

Houston had decided to abandon the Alamo and to concentrate all his forces, so they would not be defeated in small groups by Santa Anna's large army. The Alamo troops, however, under the command of Colonel William Travis, decided to remain at their posts. They numbered about one hundred eighty, including two famous frontiersmen—Jim Bowie and Davy Crockett. These were men of the West. For them, the coming battle at the Alamo was an opportunity to help Texas win its independence. They regarded the Alamo as a place of honor, where they were prepared to die. As Santa Anna's forces laid siege to the Alamo, Colonel Travis issued an appeal for reinforcements. His appeal ended with the following words: "If this call is neglected I am determined to sustain myself as long as possible and die like a soldier who never forgets what is due his honor and that of his country. VICTORY OR DEATH."[11]

Travis's appeal was heard. In many parts of America, money and soldiers were raised and sent on their way to Texas. Unfortunately, it was too little, too late to help Travis and the men of the Alamo. Over the next few days, Santa Anna's troops inched closer and closer to the walls of the Alamo. Their shells pounded the old mission's decaying walls, making its defense

The Mexican Army killed all the Texans who defended the Alamo in the war for Texan independence. However, the battle gave Sam Houston time to gather his troops before facing Santa Anna.

more and more difficult. Travis asked Houston for assistance, but the general had too few men to stand up to Santa Anna's huge army.

Finally, in the dawn hours of March 6, 1836, Santa Anna unleashed a massive attack against the Alamo. Advancing in several columns, his men were repeatedly beaten back, but the defenders could hold their positions no longer. The Mexicans streamed into the Alamo. Vowing to spare none of the enemy, they massacred all the Texan troops. A short time later, another Mexican army defeated a force of Texans near Goliad, south of the Alamo and San Antonio. Under Santa Anna's orders, most of the survivors of this battle were massacred, too.

Houston versus Santa Anna

As far as General Santa Anna was concerned, the war against the Texans was now over. He divided his forces into several units and ordered them to destroy every town and plantation in their path. Sam Houston, knowing that his small army was no match for Santa Anna, retreated to the east.

In March, Texas had declared itself independent and established a capital at Washington-on-Brazos, northeast of San Antonio. Now it looked as if this newly independent state would die almost before it had been born. The president of Texas, David Burnet, urged Houston to stand and fight: "Sir: the Enemy are laughing you to scorn. . . . You must fight them. You must retreat no farther. The country expects you to fight. The Salvation of the country depends on you doing so."[12]

Santa Anna's decision to divide his army had given Houston a slim possibility of defeating the Mexican forces. The column commanded by Santa Anna himself numbered no more than Houston's one thousand men. This would mean that the Texans could meet Santa Anna on equal terms.

During April, Houston continued his retreat, crossing the Brazos and heading east. Then he received word that Santa Anna was heading in his direction along the San Jacinto River. On April 19, the two armies clashed in a brief skirmish. Then Santa Anna withdrew to rest his men.

That night, he was joined by General Cos, whose men increased the Mexican forces. Now they outnumbered the Texans. The next day, as Santa Anna's army continued to rest, Houston led his men in an attack on their camp. Yelling "Remember the Alamo," the Texans caught the Mexicans completely by surprise. In a short battle, more than eight hundred of the Mexicans were killed or wounded. The rest surrendered. Santa Anna was taken prisoner. A few weeks later, he signed a peace treaty with Texas. He promised to withdraw his army south of the Rio Grande and to recognize that Texas had become independent.

From Independence to Statehood

In September 1836, Sam Houston was elected president of Texas. The voters of Texas wanted the territory

In the Battle of San Jacinto, Texans under the command of Sam Houston defeated troops under Santa Anna, ending the war for Texan independence.

to be admitted to the United States. President Andrew Jackson favored the admission of Texas, but there was strong opposition to it in the North. Led by Congressman John Quincy Adams of Massachusetts, Northern politicians wanted to prevent the admission of another slave state. They feared that slavery would continue to expand in the United States and wanted to prevent the growth of an institution many regarded as morally evil.

Texas remained an independent republic under the Lone Star flag for the next nine years. During that time, Texas was granted diplomatic recognition by France, Great Britain, and the United States.

His brave battle against Santa Anna for Texan freedom made Sam Houston a hero. He later became president of Texas.

In Washington, however, John Tyler—who became president in 1841—was becoming concerned that the British were acquiring too much influence in Texas. Great Britain had developed strong trading ties with Texas. Tyler also feared that Great Britain wanted Texas to remain independent so it could serve as a barrier, preventing any more westward expansion that might increase the power of the United States.

In 1844, Tyler approved a treaty with Texas, calling for it to be annexed to the United States. However, the treaty was defeated by the Senate, which wanted to prevent another slave state from entering the Union. Thus the issue of Texas annexation became a major issue in the 1844 presidential campaign. Democratic candidate James Polk supported Texas annexation. His victory indicated that popular opinion favored annexation, too. Therefore, Tyler decided to introduce a bill calling for Texas to be admitted to the Union. The bill was passed in February 1845, shortly before President Tyler's term expired. Later that year, Texas became the twenty-eighth state.

America's frontier continued to move westward.

OREGON

The Democrats wanted more than just Texas. During the election of 1844, one of the slogans used by the Democrats was "Fifty-Four Forty or Fight." It referred to a line of latitude—imaginary parallel lines running east to west across the globe—at 54°40', north. Democrats wanted this line to become the northern boundary of the Oregon Territory.

Oregon included a magnificent stretch of land larger than the original thirteen United States. Through Oregon ran huge mountain ranges, including the Cascades and the Blue Mountains, and mighty rivers such as the Snake and the Columbia. There were also fertile valleys along the Willamette River where settlers could establish farms.

The Oregon Territory was claimed jointly by the United States and Great Britain. But many Democrats were prepared to fight to make it exclusively their own. The Democratic party supported westward expansion at almost any price, including war. Their opponents, the Whigs, however, believed that a war would never be justified to gain territory on the Pacific Coast. They argued that the United States was already large enough and did not need any more territory for expansion.

In their platform of 1844, the Democrats stated: "*Resolved*, That our title to the whole of the territory of Oregon is clear and unquestionable; that no portion of the same ought to be ceded to England or any other power. . . ."[1] That territory included the present-day states of Oregon, Washington, Idaho, part of Montana and Wyoming, as well as the present-day Canadian province of British Columbia. Many Americans felt it was part of their Manifest Destiny to occupy this land and stretch the borders of the United States all the way from the Atlantic Ocean to the Pacific Ocean.

Lewis and Clark Explore the Oregon Territory

Shortly after President Thomas Jefferson completed the Louisiana Purchase in 1803, he sent the Lewis and Clark expedition west to explore the new lands that the United States had acquired. In 1803, the expedition started out near St. Louis in what is now Missouri on boats and headed up the Missouri River. Eventually, Lewis and Clark crossed into the Dakotas and climbed through the Rocky Mountains.

Their journey took them beyond the borders of the territory included in the Louisiana Purchase. The explorers continued heading west because Jefferson hoped they would find a water route—the legendary Northwest Passage—from the Mississippi River to the Pacific. In Montana, they met the Nez Percé tribe of

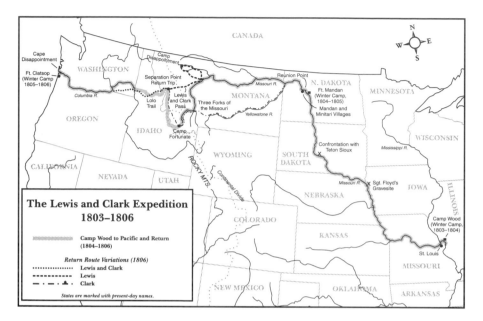

Lewis and Clark traveled from Missouri all the way to the Pacific Ocean in the Oregon Territory on a trip of exploration following the Louisiana Purchase.

American Indians, who befriended the explorers and gave them canoes to carry their men along the Columbia River to the coast of the Pacific Ocean. Here, the expedition spent the winter of 1805 to 1806, before heading east, back to St. Louis.

After the expedition returned home in 1806, Meriwether Lewis reported to President Jefferson that there was no direct water route to the Pacific Ocean from the Mississippi River. The Northwest Passage did not exist. However, the expedition still had an important impact on American public opinion. For the first time, Americans began to think about the Louisiana and Oregon territories as places where they might

Meriwether Lewis (right) and William Clark (left) brought valuable information about the West and the route to the Pacific for President Thomas Jefferson.

travel and eventually establish new settlements. Lewis also reported that Oregon would be an excellent place to set up a lucrative fur trade. The land was teeming with beaver and sea otter.

The Fur Trade

The opportunities in Oregon appealed to New York merchant and land speculator John Jacob Astor. In 1811, Astor's Pacific Fur Company established a trading post called Fort Astoria at the mouth of the Columbia River. The Pacific Fur Company expected to compete with British traders who were already established in the area.

SOURCE DOCUMENT

AT A DISTANCE OF TWENTY MILES FROM OUR CAMP WE HALTED AT A VILLAGE. . . . WE HAD NOT GONE FAR FROM THIS VILLAGE WHEN THE FOG CLEARED OFF, AND WE ENJOYED THE DELIGHTFUL PROSPECT OF THE OCEAN; THAT OCEAN, THE OBJECT OF ALL OUR LABOURS, THE REWARD OF ALL OUR ANXIETIES. THIS CHEERING VIEW EXHILARATED THE SPIRITS OF ALL THE PARTY, WHO WERE STILL MORE DELIGHTED ON HEARING THE DISTANT ROAR OF THE BREAKERS. WE WENT ON WITH GREAT CHEERFULNESS UNDER THE HIGH MOUNTAINOUS COUNTRY WHICH CONTINUED ALONG THE RIGHT BANK; THE SHORE WAS HOWEVER SO BOLD AND ROCKY, THAT WE COULD NOT, UNTIL AFTER GOING FOURTEEN MILES FROM THE LAST VILLAGE, FIND ANY SPOT FIT FOR ENCAMPMENT. AT THAT DISTANCE, HAVING MADE DURING THE DAY THIRTY-FOUR MILES, WE SPREAD OUR MATS ON THE GROUND, AND PASSED THE NIGHT IN THE RAIN.[2]

Lewis and Clark wrote extensive journals during their trip to the Pacific. Here, Lewis describes their experience upon reaching the Pacific coast.

Beaver and otter pelts, collected by the local Indians, were traded for rum, beads, and guns. Some of the furs were then shipped directly east. Other furs, however, were sent to China. They were traded for silk, tea, and porcelain. These items were carried back to America and sold at large profits.

Unfortunately, Fort Astoria did not last long enough to be very successful. The fort at Astoria was taken over by the British during the War of 1812.

Although American merchants continued to trade in the Oregon Territory, most of the trading was carried on by Great Britain's huge Hudson's Bay Company. The company had been established during the seventeenth century. Its trappers covered a huge territory across western Canada, southward into Oregon. Company traders offered better and less expensive trade goods than their American rivals. The company drove many American traders out of business.

Claims to the Oregon Territory

Nevertheless, the United States continued to lay claim to the region, along with Great Britain. Meanwhile, two other countries that had explored Oregon—Spain and Russia—decided to give up their claims. It was too difficult for these far-off nations to defend North American claims. Spain withdrew to the south into California, and Russia to the north into Alaska.

The British government offered to split Oregon, giving the United States the land south of the forty-ninth parallel to the Columbia River, then along the Columbia to the Pacific Ocean. This deal would have denied the United States valuable harbors on the Strait of Juan de Fuca and the Puget Sound, north of the Columbia River. The American government believed these harbors would play a key role in the trade with China. Therefore, in 1818, Great Britain and the United States agreed that the Oregon Territory would be jointly occupied. It would be open to settlers and traders from both countries. The agreement between

Great Britain and the United States was renewed in 1827.

American Settlers Arrive

During the 1820s and early 1830s, Americans tried to establish trading ventures and colonies in Oregon. They had little success. In the meantime, missionaries also began arriving to preach Christianity to the Indians. Americans believed it was their duty to bring Western ideas and religion to the Indian tribes, whom they regarded as "inferior" to whites. Manifest Destiny meant not only expanding geographically, but also spreading American culture across the continent.

The Nez Percé, who had helped Lewis and Clark, had already sent ambassadors to St. Louis in 1831 to express an interest in learning more about Christianity. In 1834, Methodist missionaries Jason and Daniel Lee came to Oregon. They were followed by Presbyterian minister Henry Parker, who preached to the Nez Percé. One of the most famous missionaries was Dr. Marcus Whitman. He went west across the Rocky Mountains along with his wife, Narcissa. Whitman charted a path west into the rugged Dakotas and through the mountain passes that would eventually become part of the famous Oregon Trail. When he arrived in Oregon, he preached to various tribes, including the Cayuse, the Nez Percé, and the Walla Walla.

In 1837, the United States was gripped by a terrible economic depression. Many people in the East lost their farms and businesses. As a result, they were looking for an opportunity to make a fresh start somewhere else. Reports had already come from the West about the lush farmland in the Willamette Valley of Oregon. But to reach that land required a long journey through an unknown wilderness. No matter how hardy a pioneer might be, he hesitated to risk his own life and the lives of his family on a long trek westward. Along the way, they might meet hostile American Indians, wild animals, and impassable rivers and mountain ranges. Making the trip required a bold leap. Nevertheless, some Americans decided to do it, beginning a great migration to the Pacific Coast.

Along the Oregon Trail

Small bands of pioneers gradually began arriving by wagon in Oregon during the early 1840s. Then, in 1843, a large wagon train of one thousand settlers embarked from Independence, Missouri, on the journey to the West. One of the leaders was Dr. Whitman, who had gone back east to gather more support for his missions in Oregon. The settlers carried all their belongings in about sixty wagons and herded their farm animals with them.

The trail covered about two thousand miles. It ran along the Platte River to a trading post at Fort Laramie in the present-day state of Wyoming. Travelers then crossed the Rocky Mountains at South Pass and continued to Fort Hall and Fort Boise, two of the posts maintained by the British Hudson's Bay

Thousands made the difficult journey over the Oregon Trail, hoping to find more land and better opportunities in the American West.

Company. The expedition was then forced to blaze a trail through the Blue Mountains in Oregon. At the Cascade Mountains, the wagons could go no farther. The route was too steep. Instead, the pioneers left the wagons behind and floated on rafts down the Columbia River. Some of them drowned and most of their belongings were lost. Nevertheless, approximately eight hundred seventy-five out of Whitman's original one thousand pioneers eventually reached the Willamette Valley.[3]

Later expeditions cut a new route through the Cascade Mountains. Joel Palmer, who came to Oregon in 1845, was on one of these expeditions. Not long after Palmer left Independence, Missouri, the wagon train in which he traveled met a group of American Indians who drove off their cattle. As Palmer later wrote, "*rifles* were grasped, and *horses* were hastily mounted, and away we all galloped in pursuit. Our two thousand head of cattle were now scattered over the prairie, at a distance of four or five miles from camp." Eventually, they came to an Indian village. There, they expected to find the men who had run off the cattle. But the Indians claimed to know nothing of the theft. Palmer and his companions believed them. The cattle were never found.[4]

Eventually, Palmer's party reached Fort Laramie, maintained by the North American Fur Company. Palmer described it as being made of adobe—sun-dried clay bricks—with stores and offices. Here, they traded with the Indians. Most of the tribes were friendly to the settlers.

Palmer's party continued west, until it reached the Cascades in October. It was snowing there. The trail was difficult to find. "After traveling four miles through the fresh snow," Palmer wrote, "we came to where the trail turned down to the [river]. . . . We were glad to get out of the snow, as we wore moccasins, and the bottoms being worn off, our feet were exposed."[5]

Finally, in November 1845, Palmer reached the settlement at Oregon City on the Willamette River, the capital of the new territory. Oregon City already included a Methodist and Catholic church, sawmills, taverns, blacksmiths, lawyers, and three tailor shops.

WE WERE LATE BREAKING UP OUR CAMP ON THE FOLLOWING MORNING, AND SCARCELY HAD WE RIDDEN A MILE WHEN WE SAW, FAR IN ADVANCE OF US, DRAWN AGAINST THE HORIZON, A LINE OF OBJECTS STRETCHING AT REGULAR INTERVALS ALONG THE LEVEL EDGE OF THE PRAIRIE. AN INTERVENING SWELL SOON HID THEM FROM SIGHT, UNTIL, ASCENDING IT A QUARTER OF AN HOUR AFTER, WE SAW CLOSE BEFORE US THE EMIGRANT CARAVAN, WITH ITS HEAVY WHITE WAGONS CREEPING ON THEIR SLOW PROCESSION, AND A LARGE DROVE OF CATTLE FOLLOWING BEHIND. . . . AS WE APPROACHED, THEY GREETED US WITH THE POLISHED SALUTATION, "HOW ARE YE, BOYS? ARE YE FOR OREGON OR CALIFORNIA?"[6]

In this account, a traveler describes his experience on the Oregon Trail.

By the time Palmer arrived, about five thousand settlers had already come to Oregon.[7] Settlements were expanding, and farmers were harvesting crops of wheat, potatoes, and barley. The settlers had established a government with its own legislature and a governor, George Abernethy. The government had also passed laws outlawing slavery. When James K. Polk became president in 1845, he resolved to end the boundary dispute with Great Britain permanently and make sure that Oregon became part of the United States.

Settling the Oregon Question

At first, Polk publicly proclaimed that Americans had a right to claim Oregon. But he did not specify whether he meant the line at 54°40'. However, in private communication with the British government, Polk said that he would accept a boundary line at the 49th parallel.

The British rejected Polk's offer. They wanted a boundary along the Columbia River, which was farther south. Polk was extremely irritated. He wrote in his diary that the British government had turned down his offer "in language, to say the least of it, scarcely courteous or respectful. . . ."[8]

Polk decided he would not retreat from his position. As he said to one member of Congress, "The only way to treat John Bull [a nickname for Great Britain] was to look him straight in the eye. . . ." Polk considered "a bold & firm course on our part" the best one.[9] Polk was warned by Secretary of State James Buchanan that such a course might lead to war. Polk was not afraid of this possibility. As the president wrote in his diary, he told Buchanan, "the United States will stand in the right in the eyes of the whole civilized world, and if war was the consequence England would be in the wrong."[10] Polk firmly believed that the United States had a right to the Oregon Territory at least as far north as the 49th parallel. In a message to Congress on December 2, 1845, Polk took a firm stand against the British. He recommended that the agreement for joint occupation of Oregon with Great Britain be ended. This was bound to anger the British government and might lead to conflict.

In Congress, however, there was strong support for settling the Oregon question peacefully. Southern Democrats depended on England as a market for their cotton. They did not want to see this market closed. The other major political party, the Whigs, also wanted to see the Oregon controversy settled peacefully.

Polk had gambled on taking a strong position. He believed that it was the only way to force Great Britain to the bargaining table and agree to a settlement along the 49th parallel. The British were anxious to avoid a war. In Oregon, the supply of fur-bearing animals was rapidly declining. In addition, there were very few English settlers in the area, only about one eighth the population of Americans.[11] In 1846, the British agreed to settle the dispute. They accepted a boundary line at the 49th parallel. In June, the United States Senate voted in favor of the proposal.

Meanwhile, another event had occurred that would be of enormous significance to Manifest Destiny. War had broken out with Mexico. This war would decide the fate of California and the southwestern border of the United States.

CALIFORNIA AND THE COMING OF WAR

In 1833, author Richard Henry Dana dropped out of Harvard College and boarded the merchant ship *Pilgrim*. Dana's journey took him from Boston Harbor, around the tip of South America at Cape Horn, and on to California. Very few Americans had ever seen California in the 1830s. As Dana entered the bay of Monterey, California, he wrote:

> The shores are extremely well wooded . . . and as it was now the rainy season, everything was as green as nature could make it—the grass, the leaves, and all; the birds were singing in the woods, and great numbers of wild fowl were flying over our heads. . . . the town lay directly before us, making a very pretty appearance, its houses being of white washed adobe. . . . The red tiles too, on the roofs, contrasted well with the white sides and with the extreme greenness of the lawn, upon which the houses—about a hundred in number—were dotted about, here and there, irregularly.[1]

The Growth of California

Monterey was the capital of California. The town had expanded from a mission set up there in 1770 by the

Franciscan priest Junípero Serra. Father Serra had come to California a year earlier as part of a Spanish expedition. The expedition had come to take control of the area claimed by Spain, to keep it from falling into the hands of British or Russian traders who were pushing down from the north. Father Serra established a chain of missions that stretched from San Diego to San Francisco. Each mission included a church and housing for the priests. There was sometimes a *presidio*—a small fort—for soldiers at or near the mission for defense. Each mission also had an American Indian village attached to it. One of Father Serra's primary goals was to convert the Indians to Christianity and to train them in the skills of farming. But many Indians who lived at the missions were forced to work long hours. Many were also exposed to new diseases. Some became ill and died.

By the early nineteenth century, the missions had established large wheat fields, fertile vineyards of grapes, and enormous herds of cattle and sheep. In addition, a few Mexican settlers had migrated to California. Some of them went to Los Angeles, in southern California, which became the most populous town. A few also received huge land grants to build *haciendas*—large estates—and graze their herds. By the 1830s, there were fewer than eight thousand settlers in California.

Dana's ship, the *Pilgrim*, was a trading vessel from the United States. It had come to purchase hides and tallow—the dried fat of cattle. The hides would be taken back to New England to make shoes and harnesses. The tallow would be used to make soap and candles.

While in Monterey and other ports, the *Pilgrim* sold goods brought from Boston. Because California was isolated from the rest of Mexico, Californians had little opportunity to buy items such as clothing, jewelry, and furniture. As Dana described it, people came out to the *Pilgrim* to make their purchases:

> We had spirits [liquor] of all kinds (sold by the cask), teas, coffee, sugar, spices, raisins, molasses, . . . cutlery, clothing of all kinds, boots and shoes . . . calicoes and cottons . . . silks . . . shawls, scarfs, jewelry, and combs for the women; furniture; and, in fact, everything that can be imagined. . . .[2]

In 1840, after Dana returned to Boston, he published a book about his voyage to California called *Two Years Before the Mast*. Some people who read it were so excited by his glowing description of California that they decided to move. The United States was suffering through a severe economic depression during the late 1830s and early 1840s. Many people lost their farms and businesses. Some saw California as a place to start fresh. It seemed to provide the same opportunities as Oregon. Some settlers went west along the Oregon Trail, then headed south to California after they passed Fort Hall in present-day Idaho. Then they made the journey over the Sierra Nevada Mountains into the Sacramento Valley.

Along the Sacramento River, a thriving settlement had been established by a Swiss merchant named John

Sutter. He had been a successful trader in New Mexico. Then, in 1840, the Mexican government had given him more than forty-eight thousand acres on the Sacramento River. Sutter built a fort and sent an agent to Fort Hall to persuade settlers to come to his colony at New Helvetia.

By 1846, approximately eight hundred settlers had come to California. Meanwhile, the United States government had been making efforts to buy California from Mexico. American political leaders were especially interested in the harbor at San Francisco. It seemed to be an excellent port for trade with China and Japan. Writing about San Francisco Bay, Richard Henry Dana said:

> If California ever becomes a prosperous country, this bay will be the centre of its prosperity. The abundance of wood and water; the extreme fertility of its shores; the excellence of its climate, which is as near to being perfect as any in the world; and its facilities for navigation, affording the best anchoring-grounds in the whole western coast of America—all fit it for a place of great importance.[3]

The United States government recognized the importance of California and especially the harbor at San Francisco. President Polk was prepared to offer Mexico $25 million for California. However, the Polk administration had already decided on another course of action—if the offer were turned down.

Thomas Larkin, a leading merchant in Monterey, California, had been appointed a special ambassador from the United States to California. Larkin received a confidential message from Secretary of State James

Buchanan. It urged him to lend his support to any effort by the Californians to assert their independence. He was also to tell them that, if they became independent, the United States would welcome them into the Union. Thus, the Polk administration was hoping that Californians would follow the same road that Texans had taken to independence and statehood.

Frémont and Independence

During this period, the United States government was sending out expeditions to map and explore the territories west of the Mississippi River. Captain John Charles Frémont was ordered to lead one of these expeditions. He explored the streams running east from the Rocky Mountains, the Great Basin in present-day Utah, and the Sierra Nevada Mountains. Frémont had already led two successful expeditions into the Rockies, Oregon, and California between 1842 and 1844. One of his scouts had been the famous frontiersman Kit Carson. Together, Frémont and Carson had helped map the landscape, which was still little known to most people in the East. Following the expeditions, Frémont had written about the lands he saw in such glowing terms that more settlers were persuaded to head westward.

In February 1845, Frémont set out from Bent's Fort, in the eastern part of the present-day state of Colorado, with more than sixty well-armed men. Once again, he was accompanied by Kit Carson. Although the main goal of the expedition was exploration, there

John C. Frémont, who led a government-backed expedition to explore parts of the West, went to California, where he helped settlers there fight for independence from Mexico.

may have been another purpose as well. Ever since Texas had been annexed to the United States, tensions between the Polk government and Mexico had been growing. There was a chance that war might break out. Frémont's expedition was strong enough to establish an American military presence in California should war begin with Mexico.

Frémont's expedition reached Sutter's Fort on the Sacramento River in December 1845. In January, Frémont met with Mexican Army commander General Don José Castro. Castro gave Frémont permission to spend the winter in the San Joaquín Valley. But a short time later, Castro apparently changed his mind. Frémont received a message ordering him to leave California immediately. He had moved his small band of men without permission, and Castro may have decided that the Americans were trying to defy Mexican authority.

At first, Frémont refused to leave. He and his troops created a makeshift fort out of logs and hoisted the American flag. But Castro's forces greatly outnumbered Frémont's. Frémont finally decided to abandon his fort and move north to Oregon. There, while continuing his explorations, he met Lieutenant Archibald Gillespie, who had come from Washington, D.C. Gillespie carried a secret message for Frémont. The message was delivered verbally, but, according to Frémont, it was enough to persuade him to return to California.

Frémont believed that General Castro was going to lead the Maidu Indians of the Sacramento Valley against the American settlers. Frémont struck first, attacking a number of Indian villages. The American settlers took Frémont's action as an indication that he would support them if they revolted against the Mexican authorities. On June 14, 1846, a group of militiamen under the command of William B. Ide captured the town of Sonoma, north of San Francisco. At Sonoma, the victorious settlers established the California Republic. They even hoisted a flag with a star and a bear on it. The Bear Flag Republic was born. As California was declaring its independence from Mexico, the United States and the Mexican government were preparing to go to war.

The Road to War

In 1845, as Texans prepared to join the United States, the Mexican government still insisted that Texas was part of Mexico. Mexico had gone back on the agreement made by Santa Anna during the 1830s. Fearing that Texas might be invaded, President Polk sent a force of a few thousand soldiers to Corpus Christi on the Nueces River. However, the Rio Grande was his "ultimate destination."[4] Texans claimed the Rio Grande as their southern boundary, and Polk agreed.

In command of the army at Corpus Christi was General Zachary Taylor. General Taylor was sixty-one years old and a veteran of the War of 1812. Unlike many other generals, he seemed to care nothing about his appearance. Instead of a uniform, he wore old civilian clothes and a rumpled cap. His men called him Old Rough and Ready. Polk hoped that, by putting an army on the Nueces River, he could prevent any Mexican attack. He also hoped to settle other outstanding issues between the United States and Mexico. These included the boundary line along the Rio Grande. Mexico still claimed some of the land north of the river as its own. Indeed, Mexican ranchers and farmers already occupied lands between the Rio Grande and the Nueces River and did not want to give them up.

In addition, the Mexican government owed United States citizens an estimated $8.5 million. This money was for goods sold to the government but never paid for by the Mexican authorities. Polk knew that Mexican President José Herrera had very little money to pay these claims. Polk was ready to have the United States government pay for them. But he wanted something in return: the Rio Grande as the southern boundary of Texas. Polk also wanted Mexico to give up its claims to California and New Mexico. Polk was prepared to offer $30 million for both of these territories.

In November 1845, an ambassador named John Slidell was sent to Mexico. His mission was to offer these proposals to President Herrera. Slidell had been a Democratic congressman from Louisiana, and he spoke fluent Spanish. His mission was strongly opposed by many Mexicans, however. They feared that he was trying to persuade the Herrera government to give up too much land.

Slidell spent several months in Mexico, but the Mexican president refused to meet with him. In January 1846, Polk ordered General Taylor to proceed south to the Rio Grande. This act may have been designed to put more pressure on the Mexican government. However, the Mexicans were angered by the presence of an American army on the Rio Grande. By April, Slidell still had not met with the Mexican authorities. At this point, President Polk decided that he should consider other action. Polk recommended to his Cabinet that they "take the remedy for the injuries and wrongs we had suffered into our own hands." The Cabinet agreed.[5] Polk was prepared to go to war.

The War Begins

When General Taylor reached the Rio Grande, he began building Fort Texas across the Rio Grande from the Mexican town of Matamoros. He also blockaded the Rio Grande with ships to cut off supplies that could be sent to Matamoros by sea. The Mexican government regarded the blockade as an act of war. General Pedro de Ampudia, who was in charge of Mexican forces at Matamoros, wanted Taylor to leave the area. As Ampudia put it, if Taylor did not retreat, "it will clearly result that arms and arms alone, must decide the question."[6]

Taylor did not retreat. In April, the Mexican Army crossed the Rio Grande and attacked Fort Texas. General Taylor then moved his main army against the Mexicans. He defeated them in May, driving the

SOURCE DOCUMENT

TO THE SENATE AND HOUSE OF REPRESENTATIVES:

THE EXISTING STATE OF RELATIONS BETWEEN THE UNITED STATES AND MEXICO RENDERS IT PROPER THAT I SHOULD BRING THE SUBJECT TO THE CONSIDERATION OF CONGRESS. . . .

AS WAR EXISTS, AND NOTWITHSTANDING ALL OUR EFFORTS TO AVOID IT, EXISTS BY THE ACT OF MEXICO HERSELF, WE ARE CALLED UPON BY EVERY CONSIDERATION OF DUTY AND PATRIOTISM TO VINDICATE WITH DECISION THE HONOR, RIGHTS, AND THE INTERESTS OF OUR COUNTRY. . . .

IN FURTHER VINDICATION OF OUR RIGHTS AND DEFENSE OF OUR TERRITORY, I INVOKE THE PROMPT ACTION OF CONGRESS TO RECOGNIZE THE EXISTENCE OF THE WAR, AND TO PLACE AT THE DISPOSITION OF THE EXECUTIVE THE MEANS OF PROSECUTING THE WAR WITH VIGOR, AND THUS HASTENING THE RESTORATION OF PEACE. . . .[7]

In his May 11, 1846, message to Congress, President Polk urged members to declare war on Mexico.

Mexican soldiers back across the Rio Grande. After President Polk heard about the battles along the river, he realized that war had begun. On May 11, 1846, he issued a statement. It said that "Mexico has passed the boundary of the United States, has invaded our territory, and shed American blood upon the American soil. She [Mexico] has proclaimed that hostilities have commenced, and that the two nations are now at war."[8] The Mexican War had officially begun.

5

WAR WITH MEXICO

In 1846, the United States went to war to carry out its Manifest Destiny. President Polk had no intention of conquering Mexico. It would have been impossible for the United States Army to conquer a country with a population of 7 million people, even though the United States had almost three times that many citizens. Polk simply wanted to expand the territory of the United States. This meant acquiring California and New Mexico and securing the Rio Grande as the boundary of Texas. That was why Polk had sent General Zachary Taylor to the Rio Grande. Polk knew there was a good chance that Taylor's presence would provoke a war with Mexico—and that is exactly what happened.

Taylor Faces the Mexican Army

In May, Taylor already found himself facing a strong Mexican army commanded by General Mariano Arista. This army had left Matamoros and crossed the Rio Grande. At first, Taylor was not entirely certain where the Mexicans were located. On May 8, 1846, however, the two armies finally clashed at Palo Alto, north of

General Zachary Taylor and the United States Army fought General Mariano Arista at Palo Alto. This battle began a long struggle for control over western lands.

Fort Texas. It was an indecisive battle. But the American infantry had performed well, holding its ground against a furious charge by the Mexican cavalry. General Arista withdrew his army south to Resaca de la Palma.

There, the two armies fought again on May 9. This time, Taylor's army decisively defeated the Mexicans, who fled across the Rio Grande. After the battle, Taylor returned to Fort Texas, where he found that Major Brown had been killed. He renamed the stronghold Fort Brown. It eventually became the town of Brownsville, Texas.

Decision at Monterrey

Following their defeat, the Mexican Army evacuated Matamoros. General Taylor occupied the town later in May. He did not treat its citizens as a conquered people, putting them in prison and taking their property. Instead, he wanted his army to leave the Mexicans alone, so he could win their support.

Taylor did not remain long in Matamoros. He began moving his army westward along the Rio Grande by boat to their next destination, Camargo. Soon, new recruits began arriving from the United States. Taylor's army eventually increased to twelve thousand. But disease broke out among the troops. About fifteen hundred men died before they ever had an opportunity to engage the Mexicans in battle.[1] The Americans called Camargo "a Yawning Graveyard."[2]

By early September, Taylor had finally taken his men out of Camargo. The army was heading west to its next destination—Monterrey. This heavily fortified town was a key position for the United States Army to occupy in order to control the northern part of Mexico. It was defended by General Pedro de Ampudia, who had replaced the unsuccessful General Arista. The Mexican Army numbered about ten thousand. Many of these forces were stationed within Monterrey. Some of the soldiers had also been placed in a large fortification, known as the Black Fort, that stood in front of the city. Another force occupied Independence Hill, overlooking Monterrey. Any army that controlled this position could fire its cannons down on Monterrey and control the city.

General Taylor's army approached Monterrey on September 19, 1846. Taylor saw when he got there that Independence Hill was critical to victory. He sent a force commanded by General William Worth on a flanking movement around Independence Hill to capture the position from the Mexicans.

On September 21, Taylor ordered an attack in front of the town. He hoped this would keep the Mexicans occupied while Worth took Independence Hill. Taylor's men found themselves under heavy fire and began to retreat. But one infantry unit, under the command of Captain Electus Backus, held its position until it was reinforced. The American forces then pushed back the Mexicans. Over the next two days, General Worth drove the Mexicans from Independence Hill. Then, Taylor and Worth led a combined attack on Monterrey. Fierce house-to-house fighting took place between the American soldiers and the Mexicans. As the Mexicans fell back, General Ampudia finally asked for a truce. Although his men still controlled part of the city and the Black Fort, he was ready to turn over the city to the Americans. He wanted permission to take his army out of Monterrey. Taylor agreed to let Ampudia's army leave, but without most of its weapons.

Monterrey was an important victory. But when word of Taylor's agreement with Ampudia reached President Polk, he was extremely angry. The president wrote in his diary: "In agreeing to this armistice [truce] General Taylor violated his express orders and I regret that I cannot approve his course. He had the enemy in his power and should have taken them prisoners. . . ."[3] Taylor's commanders, however, agreed with his decision. They believed that, if Taylor had continued the battle, he might have lost many more men. One of those who strongly supported General Taylor was Colonel Jefferson Davis, who led a unit of infantry from Mississippi.[4]

The Return of Santa Anna

While President Polk was directing the war against Mexico, he was also trying to bring about peace as quickly as possible. Polk wanted to keep the number of American losses in the field as low as he could. The president also had to deal with critics of the war at home. Political leaders such as John Quincy Adams believed that America was not justified in going to war against Mexico. Some Northerners also believed that Polk, a Southern Democrat, was waging war to extend the territory that would be open to slavery. Indeed, this may have been one of the reasons that Polk went to war. But his primary goal was to expand the territory of the United States so that the nation could fulfill what he believed was its Manifest Destiny.

The president's major efforts at negotiating a peace with Mexico were directed at one man—Antonio López de Santa Anna. After serving as Mexican president until 1844, Santa Anna had been kicked out of office because his administration was so corrupt. The former president was forced into exile in Cuba. From there, he began to plot his return to power. In February 1846, an ambassador from Santa Anna in Cuba arrived in Washington. The ambassador, Colonel Alejandro J. Atocha, told President Polk that, if Santa Anna returned to power, he would be willing to negotiate a settlement with the United States. Supposedly, Santa Anna's settlement would give the United States additional western territory, including Texas, New Mexico, and northern California, in exchange for $30 million. The only problem was that Santa Anna remained in exile. He was in no position to negotiate any settlement with the United States.

As the war went badly for Mexico, however, many Mexicans began to believe that they needed Santa Anna's military ability. By this time, the United States Navy was blockading the Mexican coast to prevent supplies from coming into the country. For Santa Anna to return to Mexico, he would need President Polk's permission to get through the blockade. This permission was granted. Santa Anna returned to Mexico City in September. He arrived just as Zachary Taylor was winning the Battle of Monterrey.

Contrary to his promises, Santa Anna had no intention of making a deal with the Americans. Instead, he headed north almost immediately. He hoped to avenge the defeat of General Ampudia. Gathering an army of more than twenty thousand men, Santa Anna advanced against Taylor's army.

Taylor took up a defensive position at Hacienda de Buena Vista—a rugged area with hills and gullies. Skirmishing between the two armies occurred on February 22, 1847.

The next day, it appeared that Santa Anna's forces might defeat Taylor's army. At one point, General John E. Wool, Taylor's second-in-command, said: "General, we are whipped." But Taylor refused to retreat. "That is for me to determine," he answered.[5]

Taylor sent in reinforcements, including the Mississippi infantry commanded by Jefferson Davis. Along with the powerful American artillery units, these men helped save the day, preventing the

General Santa Anna renounced his peace agreement with the United States and then fought Zachary Taylor's troops at Hacienda de Buena Vista.

Mexicans from winning a victory. That evening, both armies rested on the battlefield. Taylor went to get more reinforcements to strengthen his army and prepare for the next day's battle. But the following morning, the American soldiers awoke to find that the Mexicans had retreated. Apparently, Santa Anna did not think his army had enough supplies for another day of battle. He had headed back to Mexico City.

Kearny Moves West

As part of his plan to add more territory to the United States, President Polk directed that a small army take control of New Mexico, then move westward to California. Colonel Stephen Kearny, a fifty-two-year-old soldier and explorer, assembled a force of sixteen hundred men at Fort Leavenworth (now in Kansas). In the heat of summer, Kearny's soldiers headed west to Bent's Fort. The fort had been founded by William and Charles Bent as a trading post for Americans traveling along the Santa Fe Trail into New Mexico. They traded hardware, calico, and clothing with the Mexicans in return for beaver skins and gold. The trade brought more Americans to Mexican territory and helped persuade American political leaders that this territory should become part of the United States.

In August, Kearny was on his way to Santa Fe. He had issued a proclamation telling the Mexican people that he was coming with a large military force. New Mexico was very lightly defended by the Mexican government. Santa Fe was too far away from Mexico City

Colonel Stephen Kearny headed a small army to take control of New Mexico and California to gain more territory for the United States.

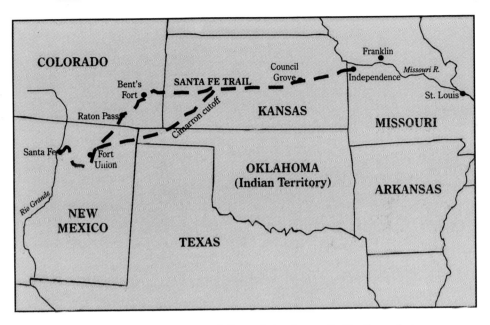

Many American settlers followed the Santa Fe Trail on their way to the West.

to be easily supplied. Therefore, as Kearny approached, Governor Manuel Armijo retreated. In August 1846, Kearny's men took control of Santa Fe, the center of New Mexico. They built a fort to defend the area and secure it as part of the United States. Kearny was now ready to complete the rest of his mission. He began marching toward California.

What Kearny did not know was that the conquest of California had already begun. On July 4, 1846, John C. Frémont had announced that he planned to take control of California from Mexico. About the same time, Commodore John Sloat—commander of the United States Pacific squadron of ships—had sailed into the bay at Monterey, California. Sloat was afraid that the British might send a fleet south from Canada and claim California for themselves. Therefore, he decided to act first. He landed about two hundred fifty men on shore. The tiny Mexican force commanded by General José María Castro fled the city. Later in July, Frémont arrived in Monterey with his own force of approximately one hundred fifty men.

After capturing Monterey, Sloat, who was already sixty-five years old, retired from the navy. He was replaced by fifty-one-year-old Commodore Robert F. Stockton. Together, Stockton and Frémont planned to complete what had been started with the victory at Monterey.

The two men sailed south from Monterey to San Diego with their troops. Along with Frémont were Arnold Gillespie and scout Kit Carson. Stockton and Frémont sailed for San Diego, which was held by a small force of Mexicans. Frémont and his men easily took control of the city after the outnumbered Mexicans fled.

The next destination was Los Angeles, the capital of Mexican California. Frémont and his men rode north from San Diego. Meanwhile, Commodore Stockton had landed his own men farther north at San Pedro. The Mexican force under General Castro was not strong enough to stop the American advance. In August, Frémont and Stockton entered the capital.

It appeared the Americans had achieved an easy victory—perhaps too easy. The Californios—Mexican residents of California—had not given up that quickly.

Commodore Robert F. Stockton (seen here) helped John C. Frémont and Stephen Kearny take over California.

Frémont had only left a small force in Los Angeles under the command of Gillespie. By September, the Californios had assembled a small army under the leadership of Captain José María Flores. Flores's troops drove Gillespie and his men out of Los Angeles. The tiny American garrisons at San Diego and Santa Barbara were also defeated. When Commodore Stockton tried to retake Los Angeles, Flores successfully defended it. Stockton then sailed south, where he retook San Diego.

This was the situation in California when Stephen Kearny, who had conquered New Mexico, arrived from Santa Fe late in 1846. Kearny planned to head for San Diego. He hoped to join Commodore Stockton there. But before his soldiers ever reached their destination, they were almost defeated by a force of Mexican cavalry in December. Fortunately, Kearny got a message through to Commodore Stockton, who sent reinforcements. The Mexicans then withdrew. Once in San Diego, Kearny and Stockton were ready to march north with their troops to retake Los Angeles.

Meanwhile, Flores had been running short of ammunition and supplies. His men were poorly trained, and they proved no match for Kearny and Stockton. In January 1847, the Americans defeated Flores near Los Angeles. The Mexican authorities signed a peace treaty, and the war in California was over. The Californios agreed to stop fighting. They became American citizens. The United States had taken control of California.

The Campaign for Veracruz

Although the United States Army was achieving success against Mexico's forces, President Polk realized that he could not allow the war to continue much longer. There would be too many casualties, and the American people would not continue to support the war. Therefore, the president and his advisors had begun thinking about a campaign aimed at the heart of Mexico.

They believed that, by capturing Veracruz—a large port city on the east coast of Mexico—or Mexico City itself, they could force Santa Anna to negotiate a peace agreement. President Polk did not want Zachary Taylor to lead such an expedition. Polk had opposed Taylor's decision to let the Mexican Army leave Monterrey. In addition, Polk thought that Taylor, a member of the Whig party, disliked the Democrats and planned to run for president in 1848.[6] He had already gained great popularity among the American people because of his victories over the Mexicans. Another such victory at Veracruz might be enough to get him elected.

Instead, Polk turned to Winfield Scott. Scott was the commanding general of the entire United States Army. Scott was a huge man—six feet four inches tall and two hundred fifty pounds. Unlike General Taylor, Scott was very fussy about his appearance. He loved to wear beautiful military uniforms. He was nicknamed Old Fuss and Feathers. Because of Scott's position, the president had considered sending him to northern

Major General Winfield Scott was in charge of the United States Army during the war with Mexico.

Mexico to command Taylor's armies just after the war began in 1846. But Scott and Polk had a heated disagreement over the conduct of the campaign. The president ordered Scott to stay in Washington, away from the battlefield. Months later, the two men had not forgotten their past differences. In the fall of 1846, however, Scott submitted a plan for the conquest of Veracruz. Polk realized that, even though he did not like the general personally, Scott was the best man to carry out the campaign.

Scott's plan called for capturing Veracruz by an amphibious landing (from the sea to the shore). It would be the largest amphibious invasion in American history up to that time. Scott organized a force of twelve thousand soldiers. To transport them to Veracruz, he acquired privately owned ships from various ports in the United States. Then he arranged to have almost one hundred fifty small boats built to carry the troops from the ships at sea to the landing beaches near Veracruz.

In early March 1847, Scott approached the Mexican coast from the sea. Although the Mexicans might have contested his landing, most of their troops stayed within the walls of Veracruz.

Once his soldiers were on shore, Scott began to set up cannons around the city. One of the engineers who scouted the Mexican defenses at Veracruz and decided where the artillery should be placed was Captain Robert E. Lee. For the rest of the month, the United States Army pounded Veracruz with cannons and

Captain Robert E. Lee aided the assault against the Mexicans at Veracruz by scouting out where artillery would overpower the Mexican defenses. His brilliant efforts later helped Lee become the commanding general of Confederate forces during the Civil War.

The American forces of General Winfield Scott landed at Veracruz with the naval help of Commodore Matthew Perry and his forces.

mortars (short cannons that launch shells into the air at high angles so they can be shot over walls). By March 27, the city had surrendered.

The Advance on Mexico City

General Scott now began to move his forces inland along the road to Mexico City. This campaign would take much longer than the siege of Veracruz. As Scott was landing on the beaches, Santa Anna was returning from his defeat at Buena Vista. He gathered an army equal in size to Scott's and set up a defensive position at a town named Cerro Gordo. At Cerro Gordo, the road ran through a narrow pass, guarded by hills and rocky cliffs. Santa Anna believed his army could stop the American advance there and prevent Scott from reaching Mexico City. Then Mexican guerrilla forces could move in behind the American forces and cut off their supply line to the coast.

Santa Anna's plan seemed to have all the elements of success. As Scott's army approached Cerro Gordo, there appeared to be no way to remove Santa Anna except by a risky frontal attack. Unknown to Santa Anna, however, there was a route around Santa Anna's flank. It had been discovered by two of Scott's engineers—Captain Lee and Lieutenant Pierre G. T. Beauregard. Scott ordered that a trail be cut through the woods. As part of his army moved around the flank, the rest would advance against the Mexicans.

American forces attacked on April 17, 1847. Although the Mexicans put up a strong defense, the flanking movement was too much for them. Santa Anna fled from the battlefield with a few men and headed back toward Mexico City. One fourth of his troops had been taken prisoner by Scott's army. Afterward, Scott told his men: "Soldiers, you have a claim on my gratitude for your conduct this day, which I will never forget."[7]

Unfortunately, some of the soldiers Scott was addressing were already getting ready to go home. They had only volunteered to serve for one year, and their time was up. They had had enough of battle. Although his army was reduced in number, Scott decided to keep moving toward Mexico City. Before the Battle of Cerro Gordo, he had left some of his troops behind to keep open his supply line to the coast.

Afterward, he brought all his soldiers forward. He had decided to let his army gather supplies from the farms and towns along the route to Mexico City. It was a risky decision. There might not be enough supplies. But Scott had decided to take the risk. He gambled that he might be able to defeat Santa Anna quickly and capture the capital of Mexico.

But it would not be easy. Mexico City lies in a valley about seven thousand feet above sea level. Lakes and marshes guard the approach to the city, with several roadways running along them. An advancing army had to move along one of these roads, which could be defended by a strong Mexican force. Before deciding which route to take toward the city, Scott ordered Lee to go on a scouting expedition. Lee believed that the most direct route was too heavily defended. He advised Scott to move his army to the south and advance from that direction.

Once Santa Anna realized which approach the American forces would be taking, he placed his men along the Churubusco River, south of Mexico City. Once again, Scott relied on a flank attack, along with a direct assault on Churubusco. It was a brutal battle fought in August 1847. Santa Anna's forces held strong positions, guarding a bridge across the river. His men battled for every inch of ground, but they finally gave way in the face of a determined bayonet charge by American soldiers.

General Scott led his men against Santa Anna along the Churubusco River in order to get to Mexico City.

The Fall of Mexico City

As Santa Anna's forces retreated, Scott continued his advance on Mexico City. The southern approaches were guarded by a series of defenses, including the huge castle of Chapultepec. The castle itself contained approximately two hundred fifty troops. Among them were young cadets from the Mexican military college. Several hundred additional Mexican troops were defending its walls. Scott reasoned that, if he could capture Chapultepec, he could enter Mexico City and end the war. But it would probably cost him many casualties.

Scott began bombarding the castle with his heavy cannons on September 12, 1847. He hoped to reduce

General Scott's attack on the castle at Chapultepec was costly for the Americans, but it ultimately won the war.

its defenses and kill many of the defenders. The next day, the assault began. A unit commanded by General Franklin Pierce of New Hampshire led the attack. After a bloody struggle, the American troops began to put their scaling ladders against the walls of the castle. The Mexicans pushed them over and shot at the Americans below. More ladders went up, and the Americans climbed in the face of withering gunfire. Eventually, they reached the top and went into the castle.

Chapultepec fell. Two days later, General Scott marched into Mexico City. With the fall of the Mexican capital, the end of the war was near.

THE RESULTS OF WAR

6

Mexican citizens had hoped that their brave troops under General Santa Anna would eventually defeat the American invaders. When Mexico City fell and American troops began taking over the city, some Mexican citizens took matters into their own hands. They formed an angry mob and began firing on the American soldiers. American troops shot back with rifles and artillery. Santa Anna was unable to come to the aid of his countrymen. He had already fled into central Mexico.

Terms of Peace

Meanwhile, a new Mexican president, Manuel Peña y Peña, was trying to negotiate peace with the United States. President Polk had sent Nicholas Trist, a special ambassador to Mexico, to make an agreement. Trist was an experienced diplomat. He had served as an ambassador to Cuba and spoke fluent Spanish. At first, Trist seemed ready to make an agreement that gave Mexico the territory between the Nueces River and the Rio Grande. When Polk heard this, he was furious.

Nicholas Trist served as special ambassador to Mexico. He signed the Treaty of Guadalupe Hidalgo, which ended the Mexican War and added 530,000 square miles of land to the United States.

The president regarded this land as part of Texas. "Mr. Trist has managed the negotiation very bunglingly and with no ability," the president wrote.[1]

In November, Trist received an order from President Polk. It told Trist to return home. Trist was to be replaced by another negotiator. Although Trist was ready to leave, the Mexican government did not want him to go. He also had the support of General Scott. Trist decided to stay, though it was a violation of Polk's orders.

On February 2, 1848, Trist signed a treaty with the Mexicans at Guadalupe Hidalgo, outside Mexico City. The Treaty of Guadalupe Hidalgo recognized the Rio Grande as the Texas boundary. It also gave the United States the territories of New Mexico and California. In return, Mexico received $15 million from the United States, and the American government agreed to pay American citizens to whom the Mexican government owed money.

Although President Polk was angry with Trist for negotiating the agreement without orders, the treaty achieved what the president had wanted. The United States' borders now lay along the Pacific Ocean and the Rio Grande. The Mexican War had added more than 530,000 square miles of territory to the United States. America's Manifest Destiny seemed fulfilled. Unfortunately, the war had also taken almost fourteen thousand American lives. Polk needed peace to silence his critics, who believed the war had been far too costly. Under the Constitution, Polk had to submit the

ARTICLE V

THE BOUNDARY LINE BETWEEN THE TWO REPUBLICS SHALL COMMENCE IN THE GULF OF MEXICO, THREE LEAGUES FROM LAND, OPPOSITE THE MOUTH OF THE RIO GRANDE, OTHERWISE CALLED RIO BRAVO DEL NORTE, OR OPPOSITE THE MOUTH OF IT'S DEEPEST BRANCH, IF IT SHOULD HAVE MORE THAN ONE BRANCH EMPTYING DIRECTLY INTO THE SEA; FROM THENCE, UP THE MIDDLE OF THAT RIVER, FOLLOWING THE DEEPEST CHANNEL, WHERE IT HAS MORE THAN ONE TO THE POINT WHERE IT STRIKES THE SOUTHERN BOUNDARY OF NEW MEXICO; THENCE, WESTWARDLY ALONG THE WHOLE SOUTHERN BOUNDARY OF NEW MEXICO (WHICH RUNS NORTH OF THE TOWN CALLED PASO) TO IT'S WESTERN TERMINATION; THENCE, NORTHWARD, ALONG THE WESTERN LINE OF NEW MEXICO, UNTIL IT INTERSECTS THE FIRST BRANCH OF THE RIVER GILA; (OR IF IT SHOULD NOT INTERSECT ANY BRANCH OF THAT RIVER, THEN, TO THE POINT ON THE SAID LINE NEAREST TO SUCH BRANCH, AND THENCE IN A DIRECT LINE TO THE SAME;) THENCE DOWN THE MIDDLE OF THE SAID BRANCH AND OF THE SAID RIVER, UNTIL IT EMPTIES INTO THE RIO COLORADO; THENCE, ACROSS THE RIO COLORADO, FOLLOWING THE DIVISION LINE BETWEEN UPPER AND LOWER CALIFORNIA, TO THE PACIFIC OCEAN.[2]

The Treaty of Guadalupe Hidalgo, of February 2, 1848, ended the Mexican War with a huge settlement for the United States.

Treaty of Guadalupe Hidalgo to the United States Senate for approval. Some senators, led by Daniel Webster of Massachusetts, opposed the treaty. They believed the United States was not justified in taking any land from Mexico. Others saw the treaty as bringing in new lands that might be open to slavery. Still others believed that the treaty should not be accepted because Trist had not been authorized to negotiate it. Nevertheless, the Senate approved the treaty in March 1848 by a vote of 38 to 14.

The Election of 1848

President Polk had decided to serve for only a single term of four years. He had made this decision in 1844 when he accepted his party's nomination. Now the Democrats wanted to renominate him for a second term as president. Polk refused. The president wrote: "I assured them that I had no desire to continue beyond the present term, and that I looked forward to the period of my retirement with sincere pleasure."[3]

Because Polk refused to run, the Democratic convention nominated Senator Lewis Cass of Michigan. The Whig party, meeting in Philadelphia, turned to one of the heroes of the Mexican War as its presidential nominee—General Zachary Taylor. A third political party, the Free-Soilers, met in Buffalo, New York. It nominated former President Martin Van Buren as its candidate. The Free-Soil party included many groups opposed to the expansion of slavery. They did not want to see slavery extended to the territory that the United States had just won in the Mexican War.

The election was extremely close. General Taylor was eventually elected, but by only one hundred forty thousand votes. President Polk, who had never forgiven Taylor for his conduct during the Mexican War, was not happy with the results of the election. Polk wrote that "he [Taylor] is wholly unqualified" with "no opinions or judgment of his own upon any one public subject, foreign or domestic. . . . The country will be the loser by his election, and on this account it is an event which I . . . deeply regret."[4]

The California Gold Rush

While the presidential election was going on, an event of possibly even greater importance was occurring in California. Early in 1848, James Marshall was building a sawmill on the American River for John Sutter, the man who had settled New Helvetia in 1840. While the mill was being built, Marshall discovered gold. He was very excited and told Sutter about it. The news quickly leaked out.

Gold seekers soon began arriving in Sacramento Valley around Sutter's Fort. One man, who operated a store at the fort, found gold and spread the word to San Francisco. According to one historian, "By the middle of June, San Francisco stood half empty, with three-quarters of the men off to the mines, most stores closed . . . the newspapers suspended, outbound ships at anchor deserted by their crews."[5]

SOURCE DOCUMENT

... I WENT DOWN AS USUAL, AND AFTER SHUTTING OFF THE WATER ..., I STEPPED INTO IT, NEAR THE LOWER END, AND THERE, UPON THE ROCK, ABOUT SIX INCHES BENEATH THE SURFACE OF THE WATER, I DISCOVERED THE GOLD. I WAS ENTIRELY ALONE AT THE TIME. I PICKED UP ONE OR TWO PIECES AND EXAMINED THEM ATTENTIVELY; AND HAVING SOME GENERAL KNOWLEDGE OF MINERALS, I COULD NOT CALL TO MIND MORE THAN TWO WHICH ANY WAY RESEMBLED THIS—SULPHURET OF IRON, VERY BRIGHT AND BRITTLE; AND GOLD, BRIGHT YET MALLEABLE; I THEN TRIED IT BETWEEN TWO ROCKS, AND FOUND THAT IT COULD BE BEATEN INTO A DIFFERENT SHAPE, BUT NOT BROKEN. I THEN COLLECTED FOUR OR FIVE PIECES AND WENT UP TO MR. SCOTT ... AND SAID, "I HAVE FOUND IT."[6]

James Marshall wrote this account of discovering gold at Sutter's Mill on January 24, 1848.

Prospectors began panning for gold in the American and Feather rivers, near Sutter's Fort. Gold had been washed down over thousands of years from the hills. They also used picks and shovels to dig into the rocks along the rivers, where they discovered more gold. In December 1848, President Polk thought the California Gold Rush was important enough to speak about it to Congress: "The accounts of the abundance of gold in that territory are of such an extraordinary character as would scarcely command belief. . . ."[7] Polk's words were carried in newspapers in the East, which ran other stories about the gold fields.

In 1849, more prospectors came to California. They called themselves forty-niners. Some came by ship from the east coast, braved the rough seas and heavy winds around Cape Horn at the tip of South America, and sailed north to San Francisco. Others traveled by a shorter sea route to Panama, crossed the isthmus by foot and canoe, and sailed by ship to California. Still others traveled overland, following parts of the old Oregon Trail, then headed south to the gold fields. More than eighty thousand emigrants arrived in 1849.[8] Along the way, some of the forty-niners sang:

> *Oh California!*
> *Thou land of glittering dreams,*
> *Where the yellow dust and diamonds, boys,*
> *Are found in all thy streams!*[9]

Men sold their homes and farms to pay their way to California, where they hoped to get rich. They lived in dirty tent villages while looking for gold. Very few made a fortune. One man, named William Swain, who arrived in 1849, decided to cash in the five hundred dollars' worth of gold dust he had found and return to his home in northern New York.[10] However, many others remained in California, even if they did not find gold. They worked in stores or settled on farms, swelling the western population.

The West and Slavery

As the number of people in California grew, political leaders realized that they needed to create a government for the area. California towns were very rowdy. A government would pass laws and help protect the people who had moved to the new towns.

A government had already been established in Oregon. In 1848, Oregon became a territory—which was usually the first step toward becoming a state. The voters in Oregon had elected a territorial legislature, and the president had appointed a territorial governor. Among other things, the Oregon legislature had voted to outlaw slavery.

Meeting in Monterey in September 1849, California leaders drew up a series of laws that would form the foundation of their government. Like the settlers in Oregon, Californians also voted to keep slavery out.

This decision came at a time when a fierce debate was raging in Congress over the future of slavery. During the 1830s and 1840s, opposition to slavery had grown in the North. People known as abolitionists were calling for an end to slavery throughout the United States. Among the leading abolitionists was William Lloyd Garrison, who ran a newspaper called *The Liberator*. In *The Liberator*, Garrison called on the South to end slavery. Although abolitionists were not popular, even in the North, Southerners reacted even more strongly against the efforts of the abolitionists. Southerners viewed slavery as the basis of their plantation economy. Slaves, the South believed, were essential to running the cotton plantations. And cotton was America's largest export. In England, the biggest customer for Southern cotton, huge mills turned cotton into cloth. Southerners had made a huge investment in their slaves. This investment would be lost through abolition. In addition, slaves were routinely bought and sold among plantations throughout the South, often at large profits to the slave owners.

Southerners felt that their institution of slavery would be protected as long as there was a balance of power between slave states and free states in Congress. In 1849, there were fifteen free states and fifteen slave states. But the acquisition of new territories as a result of the Mexican War raised the issue of whether slavery should be allowed in these areas.

During the war, Congressman David Wilmot of Pennsylvania had introduced a plan calling for slavery to be outlawed in any territories acquired by the Mexican War. Called the Wilmot Proviso, his plan was defeated in the Senate. But the question of slavery in the territories did not go away. Most Northern states supported the Wilmot Proviso. The South, on the other hand, saw it as an effort to tip the balance against slave interests. Southerners believed Congress had no right to decide whether a United States territory should be slave or free. Only the states themselves could decide.

President Zachary Taylor, who had been elected in 1848, tried to sidestep the issue. He suggested to the leaders of California that, instead of becoming a territory, California should apply immediately for statehood. He also wanted New Mexico to be organized as a state.

Taylor believed that, as states, they could decide for themselves whether to allow slavery. But Taylor's position was opposed by a majority in Congress, who felt that Congress, not the states, should make the decision.

The Compromise of 1850

While the Mexican War had expanded the territory of the United States, adding rich new western lands, it also set off a furious debate. Some Southern leaders were openly talking of secession—pulling their states out of the Union if slavery and the Southern economy were not protected. Many Northern leaders were just as strongly convinced that, if slavery were allowed in

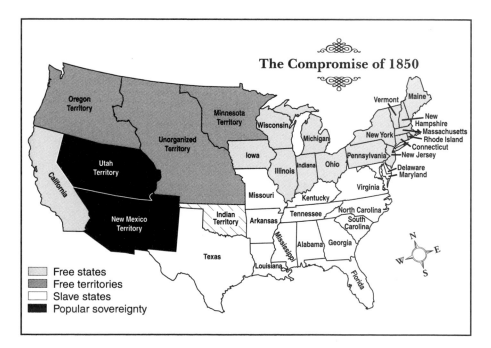

The Compromise of 1850 tried to settle slavery issues in the West by opening new territories to popular sovereignty.

the new territories, the territories would eventually become slave states and give the South too much power.

In 1850, Henry Clay, the elderly senator from Kentucky, proposed a compromise to preserve the Union. It called for California to be admitted as a free state. The rest of the new western territory would be divided between the territories of New Mexico and Utah. There, the settlers themselves could decide whether to permit slavery. This approach was known as popular sovereignty. Clay also proposed to strengthen the Fugitive Slave Law, requiring all slaves who escaped from plantations to be returned, if caught, to their owners. Finally, while slavery would continue in the District of Columbia—where the national capital was located—the slave trade there would end. Clay's compromise seemed to offer something for both the North and the South.

However, it was not enough for John C. Calhoun, a senator from South Carolina and a prominent Southern political leader. Calhoun was dying in 1850, and one of his colleagues had to deliver his speech in the Senate. Although he did not speak, Calhoun remained at his desk while his words thundered across the Senate chamber. His speech emphasized that the South had already watched its power decline as Northerners had come to dominate the federal government. If this decline did not stop, the Southern states would be prepared to leave the Union. These were terrible words that could bring an end to the United States.

Finally, Daniel Webster, the powerful senator from Massachusetts, rose. "I wish to speak to-day," he began, "not as a Massachusetts man, nor as a Northern man, but as an American. . . . I speak to-day for the preservation of the Union."[11] Webster defended the Compromise of 1850 and tried to prevent any Southern states from considering secession. Many people in Massachusetts were shocked. They had expected Webster to take a stronger position against slavery.

Meanwhile, President Taylor said he was opposed to the compromise. He thought it gave too much to the South. In 1850, Taylor died suddenly. He was succeeded by his vice president, Millard Fillmore. Fillmore supported the compromise, which was approved by the Senate. California became a free state. The South also agreed to accept the concept of popular sovereignty in Utah and New Mexico. Many Northerners, however, were enraged at the compromise. They especially opposed the Fugitive Slave Law. They saw it as an attempt to impose a harsh punishment on African Americans who had every right to be free.

The crisis of 1850 had been brought on by Manifest Destiny, the Mexican War, and slavery. The crisis had been settled and the breakup of the Union had been avoided—but only for a while.

In 1852, two men who had fought together in the Mexican War ran against each other for president of the United States. Democrats nominated Franklin Pierce, who had led his soldiers against Chapultepec. At the Whig convention, President Millard Fillmore sought the nomination against General Winfield Scott. The balloting was close, but Scott was finally nominated. In the general election, however, he was defeated by Pierce.

THE LEGACY OF MANIFEST DESTINY

Manifest Destiny Continues

The Pierce administration continued the policy of Manifest Destiny. One place for possible expansion was the Spanish island of Cuba. It had large sugar plantations worked by gangs of slaves. Cuba might offer Southerners a territory to extend slavery. However, the Spanish government was unwilling to give up the island and the United States was unwilling to go to war to obtain it.

Meanwhile, Southern interests received a boost in 1853. James Gadsden, a Southern railroad promoter, became American minister to Mexico. He negotiated the purchase of approximately thirty thousand square miles from the Mexican government. The Gadsden Purchase forms the current southern border of Arizona and New Mexico. The United States paid $10 million for the territory, which was designed to form part of the route for a new railroad. The railroad would link the South with the Pacific. Thus, Southern trade with the West could expand.

Another railroad route was being considered across the center of the country to link the Midwest with California. Approximately fifty thousand people were moving to the West each year. A railroad seemed to be the best transportation to bring them there.[1] The territories of Kansas and Nebraska, through which the railroad would run, were inhabited by Indian tribes. At the time, the Indians and United States settlers were at peace. President Pierce succeeded in signing a series of treaties with the Indians in Nebraska. They gave up 13 million acres of land and moved westward.

In 1854, Senator Stephen A. Douglas of Illinois introduced a bill designed to set up a territorial government in Kansas and Nebraska. Douglas supported settlement in the area and the building of a railroad westward. Territorial governments would organize Kansas and Nebraska with their own legislature, laws, and territorial governor. But the Kansas-Nebraska Act again raised the issue of whether slavery should be

SOURCE DOCUMENT

BE IT ENACTED . . . THE TERRITORY OF NEBRASKA . . . WHEN ADMITTED AS A STATE OR STATES, . . . SHALL BE RECEIVED INTO THE UNION WITH OR WITHOUT SLAVERY, AS THEIR CONSTITUTION MAY PRESCRIBE AT THE TIME OF THEIR ADMISSION: . . .

AND BE IT FURTHER ENACTED, . . . THE TERRITORY OF KANSAS . . . SHALL BE RECEIVED INTO THE UNION WITH OR WITHOUT SLAVERY, AS THEIR CONSTITUTION MAY PRESCRIBE AT THE TIME OF THEIR ADMISSION: . . .[2]

The Kansas-Nebraska Act, designed to help settle disputes over the expansion of slavery to the West, actually caused so much violence that the area in question became known as Bleeding Kansas.

permitted in the new territory. If slavery were not allowed, Southerners planned to oppose the act. Douglas agreed to support the concept of popular sovereignty in Kansas and Nebraska, and the new act passed.

The Kansas-Nebraska Act, however, seemed to violate an earlier law that Congress had passed in 1820. At that time, Missouri had been permitted to enter the Union as a slave state. But Congress had decided that slavery would not be permitted in any territory in the Louisiana Purchase north of 36°30' longitude. This was the so-called Missouri Compromise. The Kansas-Nebraska Act repealed that compromise, because Kansas and Nebraska were north of the line. The

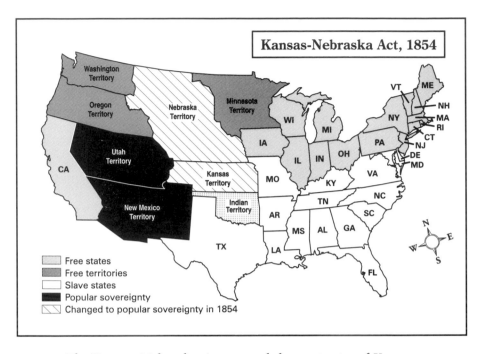

The Kansas-Nebraska Act created the territories of Kansas and Nebraska and left the question of whether they would become free states or slave states open to the vote of the people who settled there.

Missouri Compromise had stood for over thirty years and helped keep peace between the North and South. If it could be violated, then any new territory might be opened to slavery.

Many people in the North were opposed to the Kansas-Nebraska Act. Antislavery settlers moved into Kansas, where they struggled with proslavery settlers for control of the area. Soon their struggle turned violent. Popular sovereignty, which was supposed to solve the problem of extending slavery to new territories, had made the problem worse.

The Civil War

Meanwhile, the two major political parties—Whigs and Democrats—were breaking apart over the issue of extending slavery to the West. Many Whigs joined the new Republican party, which opposed the expansion of slavery. In 1856, the Republicans ran John C. Frémont as their first candidate for president. He had helped take control of California for the United States. Frémont won a large number of votes but lost the election to Democratic candidate James Buchanan.

In 1860, the Democrats could not agree on the future of slavery or on a candidate for president. The Northern wing of the party nominated Stephen

This political poster shows Captain John C. Frémont as the Republican candidate in the presidential election of 1856.

Douglas, while the Southern wing nominated John C. Breckinridge. The Republican candidate, Abraham Lincoln, was elected president because of the split in the Democratic party.

With the election of Lincoln, Southern states seceded from the Union. They feared that the future of slavery and the plantation system was jeopardized by the Republicans. Southerners thought a Republican government would force them to give up slavery. However, they believed that the principle of states' rights protected slavery and any other institution set up by state laws. They were ready to fight for these beliefs.

Many of the soldiers who had fought in the Mexican War and learned how to be battlefield commanders became military leaders during the Civil War. P.G.T. Beauregard, for example, led the Southern forces that fired on Fort Sumter in Charleston Harbor, South Carolina, in 1861. This was the opening battle of the Civil War. Former Mexican War engineer Robert E. Lee became the legendary commanding general of the Confederate forces. Others who had fought in the Mexican War included George Meade, the Union general who won the Battle of Gettysburg in 1863, and Ulysses S. Grant. It was Grant who finally defeated Lee and accepted the final surrender of Lee's army at Appomattox Court House, Virginia, in 1865.

Manifest Destiny After the Civil War

After the Union won the Civil War, the United States continued to expand its boundaries. In 1867, Secretary of State William Seward negotiated the purchase of Alaska from Russia. The United States acquired the huge territory for $7.2 million, or about 2 cents an acre. Some critics called the purchase Seward's Folly. Alaska was a large frozen area. But it was also teeming with fish, furs, and oil. Many political leaders supported the purchase because it forced Russia to leave North America, making the United States the only major power on the continent.

Meanwhile, efforts continued to link together the different parts of America. The dream of building a

Secretary of State William Seward (seated at left) and Russian diplomat Edouard de Stoeckl (standing at globe) negotiated the purchase of the Alaska Territory for the United States from Russia.

★ TIMELINE ★

1783—Treaty of Paris ends American Revolution.

1793—Eli Whitney invents cotton gin.

1794—General Anthony Wayne wins Battle of Fallen Timbers.

1795—United States and Spain sign Pinckney Treaty.

1803—President Thomas Jefferson purchases the Louisiana Territory.

1804—Lewis and Clark expedition sets out to explore Louisiana Territory.

1807—Robert Fulton launches steamboat on the Hudson River.

1811—John Jacob Astor establishes trading post at Fort Astoria.

1812—War begins between United States and Great Britain.

1814—Andrew Jackson wins Battle of Horseshoe Bend against Creek Indians.

1815—Andrew Jackson wins Battle of New Orleans.

1821—Stephen Austin selects area for settlement in Texas; Mexico becomes independent from Spain.

1825—Erie Canal opens.

1828—Andrew Jackson elected president.

1835—Texas rebels against Mexico.

1836—General Santa Anna captures the Alamo; Santa Anna defeated by Texans under Sam Houston at Battle of San Jacinto.

1837—Depression grips United States.

1840—John Sutter builds settlement on Sacramento River in California.

1843—Large wagon train heads for Oregon along Oregon Trail.

1844—James K. Polk elected president.

1845—Texas becomes a state.

1846—Mexican War begins; United States and Great Britain sign treaty establishing boundary line in Oregon Territory; California establishes Bear Flag Republic; General Zachary Taylor defeats Mexicans at Battles of Resaca de La Palma and Monterrey; Colonel Stephen Kearny occupies Santa Fe, New Mexico.

1847—General Taylor defeats Santa Anna at Battle of Buena Vista; American forces take control of California; General Winfield Scott captures Veracruz, Mexico; General Scott captures Mexico City, capital of Mexico.

1848—Mexico and the United States sign Treaty of Guadalupe Hidalgo, ending Mexican War; Zachary Taylor is elected president; Gold is discovered in California.

1850—Compromise of 1850 postpones civil war; President Taylor dies; Vice President Millard Fillmore becomes president.

1852—Franklin Pierce is elected president.

1853—United States makes Gadsden Purchase from Mexico, acquiring land in southern Arizona and New Mexico.

1854—Kansas-Nebraska Act is passed, based on concept of popular sovereignty.

1856—John C. Frémont runs as first Republican candidate for president; Democrat James Buchanan is elected president.

1860—Abraham Lincoln is elected president.

1861—Civil War rages in America.
-1865

1869—Transcontinental railroad is completed.

★ CHAPTER NOTES ★

Chapter 1: The Election of James K. Polk

1. Eugene McCormac, *James K. Polk: A Political Biography* (Berkeley, Calif.: University of California Press, 1922), p. 232.

2. Henry Steele Commager, ed., "Texas and Oregon," *Documents of American History* (New York: Appleton-Century-Crofts, Inc., 1958), vol. 1, pp. 307–308.

Chapter 2: Texas and the Western Frontier

1. Charles G. Sellers, et al., *As It Happened: A History of the United States* (New York: McGraw-Hill, 1975), p. 183.

2. Frederick Merk, *History of the Westward Movement* (New York: Knopf, 1978), p. 141.

3. Jerome Agel, *Words That Make America Great* (New York: Random House, 1997), p. 81.

4. Timothy Flint, *Recollections of the Last Ten Years,* in *The American Heritage History of the Making of the Nation, 1783–1860* (New York: American Heritage, 1987), p. 168.

5. Merk, p. 199.

6. Agel, pp. 86–87.

7. T. R. Fehrenbach, *Lone Star: A History of Texas and The Texans* (New York: Macmillan, 1968), p. 138.

8. Ibid., p. 143.

9. Ibid., p. 157.

10. Walter Lord, *A Time to Stand* (New York: Harper and Brothers, 1961), p. 69.

11. Fehrenbach, p. 208.

12. John Hoyt Williams, *Sam Houston: A Biography of the Father of Texas* (New York: Simon and Schuster, 1993), p. 147.

Chapter 3: Oregon

1. Charles A. McCoy, *Polk and the Presidency* (Austin: University of Texas, 1960), p. 44.

2. David Colbert, ed., *Eyewitness to America: 500 Years of America in the Words of Those Who Saw It Happen* (New York: Pantheon Books, 1997), p. 112.

3. Francis Russel, *The American Heritage History of the Making of the Nation, 1783–1860* (New York: American Heritage, 1987), p. 238.

4. Reuben Gold Thwaites, ed., *Journal of Travels over the Rocky Mountains* (Cleveland: Arthur H. Clark Company, 1906), pp. 40–41.

5. Ibid., p. 151.

6. Colbert, pp. 164–165.

7. Gordon Dodds, Oregon, *A Bicentennial History* (New York: W. W. Norton, 1977), p. 90.

8. Allan Nevins, ed., *Polk: The Diary of a President, 1845–1849* (London: Longmans, Green and Co., 1952), p. 2.

9. McCoy, p. 89.

10. Nevins, p. 3.

11. Russel, p. 258.

Chapter 4: California and the Coming of War

1. Richard Henry Dana, *Two Years Before the Mast* (New York: Random House, 1936), p. 73.

2. Ibid., pp. 78–79.

3. Ibid., p. 243.

4. Eugene McCormac, *James K. Polk: A Political Biography* (Berkeley, Calif.: University of California Press, 1922), p. 375.

5. Allan Nevins, ed., *Polk: The Diary of a President, 1845–1849* (London: Longmans, Green and Co., 1952), p. 70.

6. McCormac, p. 412.

7. Henry Steele Commager, ed., *Documents of American History* (New York: Appleton-Century-Crofts, Inc., 1958), vol. 1, pp. 310–311.

8. McCormac, p. 414.

Chapter 5: War With Mexico

1. John S. D. Eisenhower, *So Far From God: The U.S. War With Mexico 1846–1848* (New York: Random House, 1989), pp. 109–110.

2. Francis Russel, *The American Heritage History of the Making of the Nation, 1783–1860* (New York: American Heritage, 1987), p. 264.

3. Allan Nevins, ed., *Polk: The Diary of a President, 1845–1849* (London: Longmans, Green and Co., 1952), p. 155.

4. Eisenhower, p. 150.

5. Ibid., p. 188.

6. Nevins, p. 174.

7. Eisenhower, pp. 283, 293.

Chapter 6: The Results of War

1. Allan Nevins, ed., *Polk: The Diary of a President, 1845–1849* (London: Longmans, Green and Co., 1952), p. 272.

2. Paul Halsall, "Modern History Sourcebook: The Treaty of Guadaloupe Hidalgo, 2 Feb 1848," *Modern History Sourcebook*, July 1998, <http://www.fordham.edu/halsall/mod/1848hidalgo.html> (February 16, 2000).

3. Nevins, p. 298.

4. Ibid., p. 352.

5. J. S. Holliday, *The World Rushed In: The California Gold Rush Experience* (New York: Simon and Schuster, 1981), p. 35.

6. David Colbert, ed., *Eyewitness to America: 500 Years of America in the Words of Those Who Saw It Happen* (New York: Pantheon Books, 1997), p. 171.

7. David Lavender, *California: A Bicentennial History* (New York: W. W. Norton, 1976), p. 55.

8. Ibid., p. 59.

9. Holliday, p. 92.

10. Ibid., p. 409.

11. Walker Lewis, ed., *Speak for Yourself, Daniel: A Life of Webster in His Own Words* (Boston: Houghton Mifflin, 1969), pp. 401–402.

Chapter 7: The Legacy of Manifest Destiny

1. Frederick Merk, *History of The Westward Movement* (New York: Knopf, 1978), p. 383.

2. Henry Steele Commager, ed., *Documents of American History* (New York: Appleton-Century-Crofts, Inc., 1958), vol. 1., p. 332.

★ Further Reading ★

Books

Collins, Jim. *Settling the American West*. New York: Franklin Watts, Inc., 1993.

Edwards, Cheryl. *Westward Expansion: Exploration & Settlement*. Carlisle, Mass.: Discovery Enterprises, Limited, 1995.

Edwards, Judith. *Lewis and Clark's Journey of Discovery in American History*. Springfield, N.J.: Enslow Publishers, Inc., 1999.

Smith, Carter, ed. *Bridging the Continent: A Sourcebook on the American West*. Brookfield, Conn.: Millbrook Press, 1996.

Tibbitts, Alison Davis. *James K. Polk*. Berkeley Heights, N.J.: Enslow Publishers, Inc., 1999.

Internet Addresses

National Park Service. "Manifest Destiny: The Dragoon Expeditions (1843–45)." *Fort Scott National Historical Site*. n.d. <http://www.nps.gov/fosc/mandest.htm> (July 5, 2000).

PBS Online. "Manifest Destiny." *U.S.-Mexican War*. n.d. <http://www.pbs.org/kera/usmexicanwar/dialogues/prelude/manifest/manifestdestiny.html> (July 5, 2000).

White House Historical Association. "James K. Polk: Eleventh President, 1845–1849." *The Presidents*. n.d. <http://www.whitehouse.gov/WH/glimpse/presidents/html/jp11.html> (July 5, 2000).

★ INDEX ★